THE DICE CUP

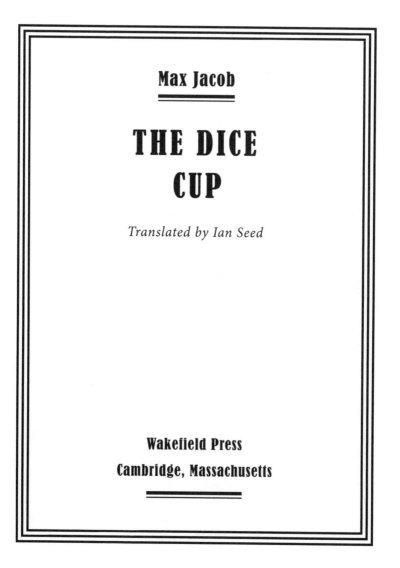

Max Jacob

THE DICE CUP

Translated by Ian Seed

Wakefield Press

Cambridge, Massachusetts

Wakefield Press, P.O. Box 425645, Cambridge, MA 02142

Originally published in French as *Le cornet à dés* in 1917.

This book was set in Minion Pro and Bernard MT Condensed by Wakefield Press. Printed and bound by McNaughton & Gunn, Inc., in the United States of America.

ISBN: 978-1-939663-86-3

Available through D.A.P./Distributed Art Publishers
75 Broad Street, Suite 630
New York, New York 10004
Tel: (212) 627-1999
Fax: (212) 627-9484

10   9   8   7   6   5   4   3   2   1

CONTENTS

FIRST PART

SECOND PART

THE DICE CUP: ADDE

TRANSLATOR'S INTRODUCTION

Art is a lie, but a good artist is no liar.—Max Jacob

With the publication of *The Dice Cup* (*Le Cornet à dés*) in 1917, Max Jacob modernized and redefined the prose poem for the twentieth century.[1] *The Dice Cup* was put together from prose poems that Jacob had been writing for years, most of them between 1903 and 1910. He is reported to have kept them locked away in a trunk, afraid that someone would steal them, perhaps not without good reason.[2] When the First World War broke out in August 1914, Jacob moved much of his work to a friend's house in Enghien, a small town a few kilometers north of Paris, for safekeeping. *The Dice Cup* was lucky to have survived at all. In September 1914 the Germans were so near to Enghien that most of its citizens began to evacuate. In the chaos, Jacob came close to losing all his writing.[3] With the war still raging in 1917, he finally published *The Dice Cup* at his own expense and by subscription. He may have felt pressured into this decision because he did not want to lose out to his close friend, mentee, and rival, Pierre Reverdy, who published his own *Prose Poems* in 1915, as well as an innovative novel in prose and verse, *The Thief of Talant* (*Le voleur de Talan*), in 1917.

    The Dice Cup was well received, and Jacob's work began to gain wider recognition from the 1920s onward, despite some of the efforts by surrealists and others to exclude him from the avant-garde literary canon (a point I shall return to). The recognition had been some time in coming. At this point, Jacob was already in his early forties and had been living an impoverished existence for the best part of two decades.

Max Jacob's early life is often evoked in *The Dice Cup*. He was born in the town of Quimper, Brittany, on 12 July 1876, the fourth child in a family of six brothers and sisters. Lazare Jacob, Max's father, owned a successful antiques shop. There were few Jews in Quimper at that time, and for the most part the Jacob family did not practice the Jewish religion, except to pay lip service to it on special occasions. Jacob was a bright, even brilliant pupil at high school, but was known as *le Juif* and frequently bullied. From early adolescence he was passionate about painting. He also enjoyed singing operatic songs while accompanying himself on the piano. In October 1894, at the age of eighteen, he left Quimper for Paris to enroll at the École Coloniale, the school for colonial administration, and at the Faculté de Droit, the law school. He interrupted his studies when he was called up for military service in 1896 but returned to Paris a few months later after being released from his military duties, in part because of his incompetence when it came to barracks drills and in part, perhaps, because he was Jewish. This was the time when the Dreyfus affair was attracting much public attention and dividing France, and Jews were being portrayed as unpatriotic and treacherous. Back in Paris, he left his studies for good when he was offered a position as an art critic for *Le Moniteur des arts*, to which a friend had introduced him, and for a short time he was able to make a reasonably comfortable living. In 1899, much to the disappointment of his family, Jacob abandoned this position to dedicate himself to being an artist. There would follow many years of poverty in which Jacob worked in a series of insecure and poorly paid jobs, including warehouseman, clerk, secretary, home tutor, and even babysitter.

In 1901, a meeting occurred that would change the course of his life. Walking into the Ambroise Vollard Gallery, as he happened to be passing by, he discovered the work of Pablo Picasso, not yet twenty years old and still an unknown. Picasso's paintings revealed an entirely new world of artistic possibilities for Jacob, and the two immediately became close friends. Jacob showed some of his poems to Picasso, and Picasso convinced him that his true vocation was that of poet, and that he should dedicate himself to this above all else, whatever the material consequences. They supported each other in their poverty, sharing a room with only one single bed at the Hotel Voltaire. While Jacob slept at night, Picasso painted. Then Picasso slept while Jacob went to his day job in a department store. Later he would say that Picasso "found I had talent, and I believed in him more than in myself," and, more dramatically, "Picasso told me I was a poet: it's the most important revelation of my life except for the existence of God."[4]

Through Picasso, Max Jacob met the poet André Salmon, an early defender of cubism, and, crucially, Guillaume Apollinaire,[5] both of whom were opening new routes for poetry in opposition to the vagaries of post-symbolism. Max Jacob's name appeared rarely in literary journals of the time, but he was already reading, commenting on, and judging the poems of better-known friends, and developing a writer's discipline all his own. One of his methods was to walk through the streets of Paris and try to come up with an image or a line of poetry or an idea in the distance between each lamppost. If he failed to produce anything, then he would stop at the next lamppost and wait until something came to him that he could jot down, sometimes on blank telegraph forms stolen from a post office.[6] This kind of exercise must have contributed to the concentrated language, disrupted pace, and fragmentary quality of Jacob's narratives in his poetry.

In 1909, the interior life of Max Jacob was shattered when he experienced a vision of Christ, who appeared on Max Jacob's bedroom wall in a landscape he himself had painted. Thirty years on, Jacob described his conversion from "atheist Jew" to Christian:

> I fell on my knees, my eyes filled with sudden tears. An indescribable sense of well-being descended over me, I remained motionless, without understanding. In one minute, I lived through a century. It seemed to me that everything had been revealed to me. [. . .] I felt stripped of my human flesh, and these words alone filled me: TO DIE TO BE BORN.[7]

While the conversion gave Max Jacob fresh energy and much new mystical material to draw upon for his writing, it would take him another six years before the Catholic church would finally agree to baptize him on 18 February 1915, with Picasso acting as witness. By coincidence, on that same day, seventeen of Max Jacob's prose poems would appear in English in *The New Age*, a weekly magazine published in London. They had been translated by his friend, the British writer Beatrice Hastings (1879–1943), who lived in Montmartre. These were followed by seventeen more prose poems in May. The majority of these poems were included in *Le Cornet à dés* when it was finally published in 1917.

In his preface to *The Dice Cup*, Jacob sought to summarize the poetics he had been developing over several years; to place his work in the context of French prose poetry, and to give us a definition of the prose poem, sometimes by saying what it is not; and to refute the work of some of his contemporaries and predecessors as prose poetry. His poetics can come across as paradoxical.

Jacob famously declared that the prose poem, like everything that exists, is "situated." By this he meant that we must read a prose poem as an object that has its own existence independently of its author, but is situated in relation to other prose poems and to other objects in existence. This of course does not mean that the author has no part in its creation. What the author must do is give a prose poem "style." This is the case with any form of art. We should not see literature as being any different—as being, for example, simply self-expression. According to Jacob, style is the exercise of the will to exteriorize oneself through one's "chosen means." Art will always follow certain rules of its time, and the artist, or prose poet, must be able to master these. At the same time, the true artist will be able to transcend them in order to create something unique, which is "situated"; from this we recognize the work as genuine art, not simply as something that on the one hand follows the rules, or is merely vain self expression on the other. Style gives us the sensation of a work being "self enclosed"; it exists in its own right, and it is this that excites us as spectators or readers. We should not try to compare a prose poem to "reality," in the way that we would, say, a film. Rather, we should appreciate, and be thrilled by, its aesthetic qualities. The prose poem "transplants" components of reality into a realm where we can "situate" those components in relation to one another, offering us alternative versions of reality, which in any case is not something fixed and stable, any more than one's personality is.[8] However, he also cautions us when it comes to overthinking a work of art: "Artistic feeling ceases where analysis and thought intervene: it's one thing to make someone reflect, another to arouse a feeling of beauty." And in a footnote, he reminds us that the "prose poem, in spite of the rules which style it, must be a free and living expression."

Jacob goes on to take issue with other authors of the prose poem, questioning in some cases whether what they are writing is prose poetry at all. For example, the prose poem must distinguish itself from the fable of the kind produced by Charles Baudelaire or Stéphane Mallarmé and their followers, or from pages of short poetic prose pieces like precious jewels (and here he may be taking a swipe at Reverdy),[9] and above all from the "romantic disorder" of Arthur Rimbaud. Later, for example in his "Short History of *The Dice Cup*" (1943), translated here, in his *Art poétique* (1922), and in *Conseils à un jeune poète* (1941), he would go on to explain what he was attempting to do in his own prose poetry, and the sources he drew upon.

Jacob tells us that he was writing prose poetry long before he'd heard of such a thing, offering examples from his childhood and his years living in Paris as a student. Later, when he decided that his true vocation was that of poet, "I truly set myself to seizing data from the unconscious in every possible manner: words in freedom, chance associations of ideas, night dreams and daydreams, hallucinations, etc. . . ." This may seem rather like the "romantic disorder" of Rimbaud, but Jacob always insisted on clarity, specificity, and concreteness of language,[10] even as he subverted our normal expectations of narrative and poetry, above all perhaps through the logic of dreams (though the prose poems are never merely dreams), but also through mixtures of religion and myth, literary allusions, wordplay and nonsense, absurdity and parody, fast-shifting registers of language, disguised confession, and a lyricism that both touches us emotionally and sends itself up at the same time. Even his poetics as expressed in his preface to *The Dice Cup* have more than a hint of parody. Yet the prose poems could never be reduced to intellectual exercises and games. They are full of yearning, and frequently express emotions such as self-doubt, hurt, regret, fear, and shame. Jacob reveals his own all too human flaws and invites us to recognize those flaws as our own. The prose poems seek to go beyond everyday reality and also to see the sublime in that reality, however burlesque, dis-torted, or perverse it may sometimes be. Indeed, Jacob sees the mystical within the burlesque, and vice versa. Even when the prose poems appear to be more straightforwardly realist, there is always a sense of otherworldliness, of something both true in time and fixed forever in eternity, especially in those prose poems that recall and evoke his childhood.

The title of the collection deliberately echoes Mallarmé's *Un coup de dés* (A throw of the dice), published in 1897. It sug-gests making way for chance, for whatever happens to emerge from the dice cup. However, there is nothing haphazard about the way the book is organized. Jacob painstakingly selected from the prose poems he had been writing for so many years, "marrying elements which call out to each other by virtue of their affinities, and not juxtaposing them at random. Those which tumble onto the page are truly new beings."[11]

The Dice Cup was well received, and Jacob slowly acquired a degree of recognition and fame, though it was never to make him rich. Yet at the same time, he found himself rejected by the new generation of the avant-garde that emerged after the First World War in the form of Dadaism and surrealism. The surrealist journal Littérature, edited by André Breton, Philippe Soupault, and Louis Aragon, went out of its way to demean Jacob as an author. The aftereffect was that, for several decades afterward, Jacob's role in early French modernism and his achievements as an author were severely downplayed and ignored. The fact that Jacob was actively gay,[12] Jewish, and, worst of all, a Jew who had converted to Catholicism, no doubt alienated many. In addition, Jacob is someone that we cannot put a label on, as we can with, say, André Breton or Tristan Tzara. Even his old friends rejected him. He was deeply hurt when Picasso didn't invite him to be the godfather of his son, or even bother to send him news of the birth on 4 February 1921.

At the same time, Jacob was growing weary of not being able to resist all the temptations of Paris life and apply himself to his creative work. In June 1921, he abandoned Paris to live in an unused part of a monastery in Saint Benoît sur Loire.[13] For the rest of his life he would divide his time between Saint-Benoît and Paris. In January 1939 he wrote to his friend and mentee, the poet Edmond Jabès, expressing his worries over the threat of a new war in Europe. The defeat of 1940, the Nazi Occupation of France, and the new racial laws confirmed his worst fears. Prohibited from publishing and obliged to wear the

Yellow Star, he turned to selling his gouaches and illustrating his books for collectors to make a living. He could still joke about the situation, referring to the Gestapo as "J'ai ta peau" ("I have your hide"). In January 1944, his favorite sister, Mirté Léa, was arrested and died during deportation. When the Gestapo finally came for him on 24 February 1944, he was in his room in Saint-Benoît. He reportedly remained calm, even pausing to shake hands with the small number of villagers who had gathered, and who had gradually adopted him over the years as one of their own, before stepping into the Gestapo's car. He was transported to the Dancy internment camp on the outskirts of Paris, scheduled to be deported to Auschwitz on 7 March. Friends' efforts to have him released were unsuccessful, and he died of pneumonia on 5 March. Around fifty friends—among them Reverdy and Picasso—gathered two weeks later to take part in a mass organized in his memory at the Saint-Roche church in Paris. In his will, Jacob had asked to be "buried religiously and as humbly as possible in Saint Benoît sur Loire Cemetery." His wish was finally granted in 1949.[14]

ACKNOWLEDGMENTS

My warm thanks to the editors of the following publications in which a few of these translations, sometimes in earlier drafts, first appeared: *Decals of Desire* (Martin Stannard); *The Fortnightly Review* (Denis Boyles); and *Shearsman Magazine* (Tony Frazer).

I am truly indebted to my patient and brilliant editor, Marc Lowenthal, whose close reading and suggestions have made all the difference.

My thanks to Judith Feldmann of Wakefield Press for invaluable editing.

I am grateful to my wife, Justyna, for her support and encouragement.

And infinite thanks to you, Max! Translating *Le cornet à dés*, it has often felt to me as if I were having an intimate conversation with you in a small, dark room in Montmartre. I am deeply honored by coming to know you in this way.

NOTES

1. It is worthwhile recalling that the other seminal collection of prose poems from that time is *Tender Buttons* (1914) by Gertrude Stein. Although Stein's work is very different from Jacob's, depending much more on repeated sounds and associations than on imagery and dreamscape, she was, like Jacob, attempting to parallel what cubist painters were doing on canvas, and like Jacob she was Jewish and gay. They knew each other and shared the same milieu of artists and poets.

2. See the introduction to Pierre Reverdy, *The Thief of Talant*, trans. Ian Seed (Cambridge, MA: Wakefield Press, 2016).

3. See Rosanna Warren, *Max Jacob: Art and Letters* (New York: W. W. Norton, 2020) 219–220; this is the first complete biography of Max Jacob in English.

4. Quoted in Warren, 62.

5. Apollinaire tragically died of Spanish flu in 1918, weakened by his experience of the First World War. It was a loss felt keenly by Jacob and fellow poets and artists.

6. Warren, 115.

7. See Max Jacob, "Récit de ma conversion," in Max Jacob, *Œuvres*, ed. Antonio Rodriguez (Paris: Éditions Gallimard, 2012), 1473–1479.

8. In his *Art Poétique*, Jacob famously declared, "Personality is only a persistent error." See Jacob, *Œuvres*, 1349.

9. The rivalry between Jacob and Reverdy at times grew very intense. Pierre Andreu reports that one day in 1914, Pierre Reverdy took hold of Jacob's manuscript of prose poems, walked over to the stove, mimed the act of throwing them into the flames, saying to Jacob, "Do you have a copy?" Jacob responded, "No, but I have a revolver." See Pierre Andreu, *Vie et mort de Max Jacob* (Paris: La Table Ronde, 1982), 115.

10. For example, in his *Conseils à un jeune poéte*, Jacob urges us to "make concrete! Consider this word. The abstract is impoverished and dull." But "making concrete does not mean writing populist poetry [. . .], it means placing one's voice in the belly, thought in the belly, and to speak of the sublime with the voice in the belly."

11. Michel Leiris in his foreword to *Le Cornet à dés* (Paris: Éditions Gallimard, 2003), 11.

12. Jacob is also known to have had a passionate early relationship with a woman; she makes more than one appearance in his poems as "Mlle Léonie."

13. There are obvious parallels here, of course, with Reverdy's retirement from Paris in 1926 to live in a small house in St. Peter's Abbey in Solesmes. Reverdy, too, had converted to Catholicism in 1921, with Jacob acting as his spiritual godfather.

14. For many of these details of the end of Jacob's life I have drawn upon Étienne-Alain Hubert's "Vie de Max Jacob," in Jacob, *Le Cornet à dés*, 257–263.

THE DICE CUP

I dedicate this definitive edition of

THE DICE CUP

to Princess Georges Ghika
and to Prince Georges Ghika
with the respectful homage of my devoted friendship.

Max Jacob
Rascoff, 10 August 1923

3

A Short History of *The Dice Cup*

For my friend Paul Bonet

"Oh, what a title!" said Miss Hastings (English lady writer and wife of Modigliani). "In England, you know, someone would steal it before the book came out!"

They stole something quite different! The poems were well known. People would come in the morning to 7 rue Ravignan and read the poem from the night before ... my neighbors ... Picasso, Salmon, Mac Orlan, etc.... "Think what they'll scrounge from that!" Mac Orlan would say. Indeed, when the question of publishing them came up, someone I won't name rushed to produce, under a different title (we're not in London after all), a collection which tried to be a pastiche and failed. The triumph of friends! "Beaten to it, Max!" And me to Picasso: "Is it true that X is better than me?" "You know very well that imitators are always better than inventors!" That's running with the hares and hunting with the hounds—and for the truth! It didn't stop X's book from sinking into oblivion whereas the little *Cup* lives on. It came out in two editions from Éditions Stock (small yellow books), following on from the one available by subscription, published by the author, 17 rue Gabrielle, 18th arrondissement.

I remember the letter from Albert Thibaudet, then a soldier, to the War Ministry: "It seems like every dossier has landed pell-mell on my desk." Laurent Tailhade, warned by a pal, *deigned* to comment, "Dahlias, dahlias Delilah ties." In spite of that, I've had my share of success.

I've always made up prose poems, or half-prose poems. When my five brothers and sisters and I were very small and returning in the care of the maid at night from the traveling fair, we grew very scared on the staircase when the timed light went off, and I improvised the following:

Mr. cats and Mr. thieves, if cats there be and thieves there be, Mr. cats, don't scratch me! Mr. thieves, don't scare me!

That's surely the *Cup* already . . . was I twelve or fifteen years old?

Later, as a student in Paris, I hung out with some fat rich cousins, and I came up with this:

My overcoat is my shield, my umbrella my defense, I've won 50 centimes from my enemies! And you, my lady, do you know how to dance?

I knew nothing of Jarry and Père Ubu. Besides, the question of literature still didn't figure in my life.

Later, after a few adventures, there I was employed at 137 boulevard Voltaire and in possession of a young lady; we lived at 33 Boulevard Barbés. One day I said to her: "She's so weary, the buttercups on her hat shut their eyelids." It wasn't until later still when it was established I was among poets (and quoted at the famous "Afternoon of Poets" lecture, given by Apollinaire at the Salon des Indépendants in 1907; I exaggerate, I'd been collecting prose poems for a long time) that I truly set myself to seizing data from the unconscious in every possible manner:

words in freedom, chance associations of ideas, night dreams and daydreams, hallucinations, etc. . . .

EPILOGUE TO THE SHORT HISTORY

"Why don't you do a sequel to *The Dice Cup*?" Count François de Gouy d'Arcy asked me. ("He's the only man who knows what painting is," Picasso said of him.) "Do one for me!" I got down to it and one day announced over the telephone that I had sixty pages: "Come around for dinner! And bring the sixty pages!" People read them with enthusiasm. We called some friends on the phone, and with each new arrival the pages had to be read again. After midnight, my friends had the chauffeur drive me, arms full of flowers, to 17 rue Gabrielle, where I was living then. Even a ducatoon would have served me better.

A little while after that, François telephoned me to say that he and his friend Greeley had discovered a spot near Versailles from where you could see the whole of Paris. "Come and have a bite with us, we'll show you the view!" There we were, contemplating Paris from near Versailles: "And that silvery atmosphere! . . ." "Yes," I said, "the atmosphere is the only silvery thing left in Paris!" They understood the allusion. François began moaning about his poverty and his inheritance being spirited away, etc. . . . Evening came, then night. This took place in a hotel near the Étoile. "What time is it?" asked François. "Two according to this beautiful old pocket watch." "Do you like this watch? Take it!" I donned this watch for more than ten years on national holidays and ceremonies: I attached a long gold chain to it.

Now I'm thinking of selling it! What use is it when you're living as a recluse to own jewelry (like my emerald)? It's a matter of 15,000 francs, an amount that will easily last as long as my shrinking life, and which will alleviate a few small problems.

Never would *The Dice Cup* bring in as much as its supplement.

Filibuth is of the same view, for my future buyer wants to have it as a souvenir of that novel whose subtitle is: "Filibuth or the gold watch."[1]

1943

Everything that exists is situated. Everything that is above matter is situated; matter itself is situated. Two works are unequally situated either because of their authors' spirit or because of their technique. Raphaël is above Ingres, Vigny above de Musset. Madam X is above her cousin; diamond is above quartz. Perhaps this is tied to the relationship between morale and morality? In previous times it was believed that artists are inspired by angels and that there are different categories of angels.

Buffon has said: "The style is the man himself." Which means that a writer must write with his blood. This definition is salutary, but not exactly right, it seems to me. What makes the man himself is his use of language, his sensibility; one is right to say: express yourself in your own words. One is wrong to believe that that's style. Why would one want to give style in literature a different definition from that which is used in the other arts? Style is the will to exteriorize oneself by one's chosen means. Like Buffon, we generally confuse language and style because few people need an art of the will, which is to say art itself, and because everyone needs humanity in expression. In the great artistic eras, the rules of art taught from infancy make up the canons that shape a style: artists are therefore those who, despite the rules followed since childhood, find a living means of expression. This living expression is the charm of aristocracies, that of the seventeenth century. The nineteenth century is full of writers who understood the necessity of style but didn't dare to come down from the throne which their desire for purity had built. They created limitations for themselves at the expense of life.* The author, having situated his work, can make use of all kinds of charm: language, rhythm, musicality, and wit. *Once a singer has his voice in tune, he can enjoy himself with vocal embellishments.* To understand me fully, compare the familiarities of Montaigne with those of Aristide Bruant, or the snide remarks of the gutter press rubbing shoulders with the brutalities of Bousset smashing into the Protestants.

This theory is not ambitious; it isn't new either: it is classical theory I am modestly evoking. I do not mention these names to bludgeon the "moderns" with the club of the "ancients"; these are names no one contests; if I'd mentioned others I know, you may have thrown away this book, which I don't want you to do. I would like you to read it not for a long time, but often: to be understood is to be loved. Only long works are held in esteem, yet these days it isn't easy to stay beautiful a long time. One may prefer a three-line Japanese poem to Péguy's *Eve*, which is three hundred pages, and a letter by Madame de Sévigné, full of ease, joy, and bravado, to one of those old novels made up of stitched-together plots, and which claim to have done enough to hold our attention if they have met the requirements of their kind.

Many prose poems have been written over the last thirty or forty years; few poets have understood what a prose poem is and have known how to sacrifice an author's ambitions to the formal composition of a prose poem. Dimension counts for nothing in the beauty of a work. Its situation and its style are everything. Well then, I make my case that *The Dice Cup* can satisfy the reader from both points of view.

---

* The prose poem, despite the rules that style it, must be a free and living expression.

Artistic feeling is neither a sensory act nor a sentimental one; nature would be enough to give us that. Art exists; therefore it corresponds to a need: art is properly speaking a *distraction*. I'm not deceiving myself: this is the theory that has given us a marvelous people of heroes, powerful evocations of worlds where the legitimate curiosities and aspirations of people trapped in a bourgeois existence can be satisfied. But we need to give a still wider significance to the word "distraction." A work of art is a force that draws one to it, that absorbs the available strengths of the one who approaches it. There is something of a marriage here, with the art enthusiast playing the role of the wife. He needs to be seized by a will and held. The will therefore plays the lead role in creation; the rest is just the bait in the trap. The will can only be exercised in one's choice of means, for a work of art is no more than a gathering of means, and through art we arrive at the definition that I gave style: art is the will to exteriorize oneself through one's chosen means: the two definitions coincide, and art is nothing more than style. Here style is considered to be the making use of materials and the composition of the whole, not as the language of the writer. And I conclude that artistic feeling is the effect of a thinking activity on a thought activity. I make use of the word "thinking" with regret, for I am convinced that artistic feeling ceases where analysis and thought intervene: it's one thing to make someone reflect, another to arouse a feeling of beauty. I put thought with the bait in the trap.

The greater the activity of the subject, the more the feeling caused by the object will grow: a work of art must therefore be distanced from the subject. That's why it must be *situated*. We come here to Baudelaire's theory on the element of surprise:

this theory is somewhat elementary. Baudelaire understands the word "distraction" in its most banal sense. Surprise is nothing much; what is needed is to *transplant*. Surprise charms us and impedes true creation: like all charms, it is harmful. A creator doesn't have the right to be charming until after the deed is done, when the work has been situated and styled.

Let us distinguish the style of a work from its situation. Style or will creates, that is, it separates. Situation distances, that is, it excites artistic feeling. We recognize that a work has style when it gives us the sensation that it is self-enclosed; we recognize that it is situated by the small shock we receive from it or else from the margin that surrounds it, from the unique atmosphere in which it moves. Certain works by Flaubert have style; none of them are situated. Musset's plays are situated but they don't have a great deal of style. Marllarmé's work is of the type that is situated; if Mallarmé weren't artificial and obscure, he'd be a great classic. Rimbaud has neither style nor situation: he has Baudelairean surprise; he is the triumph of romantic disorder.

Rimbaud enlarged the field of sensibility, and all poets owe him a debt, but authors of the prose poem cannot use him as a model, for in order to exist the prose poem must submit to the laws of all art, which are style or will, and situation or feeling, and Rimbaud only leads us to disorder and exasperation. The prose poem must also avoid Baudelairean and Mallarméan parables if it wants to distinguish itself from the fable. One will understand that I do not regard as prose poems those notebooks of somewhat curious impressions which my contemporaries with an excess of material publish from time to time. A page of prose is not a prose poem, even when it frames two or three lucky finds. I would consider as such those so-called finds presented with the necessary spiritual margin. In this regard, I caution authors of prose poems against those precious stones which shine too brightly and attract the eye at the expense of the whole. The poem is a constructed object and not a jeweler's shop window. Rimbaud is the jeweler's shop window, not the jewel: the prose poem is a jewel.

A work of art is to be valued in itself and not by any comparisons we can make with reality. One says in the cinema: "Yes, that's how it is!" Before a work of art: "What harmony! What solidity! What style! What purity!" Jules Renard's adorable definitions collapse in the face of this truth. They are realist works, without a real existence; they have style, but are not situated; the same charm that gives them life, kills them. I believe that Jules Renard has created prose poems beyond his definitions; I don't know them, which I regret: it's possible that he's the inventor of the genre as I conceive it. For the moment I consider as such Aloysius Bertrand, as well as the author of *The Book of Monelle*, Marcel Schwob. Both of them have style and margin: that is to say, they compose and situate. I reproach the former for his romanticism "in the manner of Callot," as he says, which, drawing our attention to colors that are too violent, veils the work itself. Moreover, he has declared he considers his pieces as the material for a work and not individual works in themselves. I reproach the latter for having written short stories and not poems, and what stories! Precious, childish, artistic! It's possible, however, that these two writers created the genre of the "prose poem" without knowing it.

Max Jacob, September 1916

FIRST PART

NOTE

The poems that refer to the war were written around 1909 and could be termed prophetic. They do not have the tone our sorrows and decency require of war poems: they date from a time that was ignorant of collective suffering. I foresaw the events. I did not foretell their horror.

Don't the flashes of lightning look like this in other countries? Someone at my parents' house was talking about the color of the sky. Are there flashes of lightning? A pink cloud was coming closer. Oh, how everything changed! My God, can it be that your reality is so alive? The house where I grew up is there: the chestnut trees pressed against the window; the prefecture against the chestnut trees; Mount Frugy against the prefecture: then only peaks, nothing but peaks. A voice cried "God!" and there was a burst of light in the darkness. An enormous body was hiding half the landscape. Was it Him? Was it Job? He was poor; he showed us his pierced flesh; his thighs were covered by a loincloth: what tears, oh Lord! He came down . . . but how? Then couples larger than life descended too. They came from the air inside crates, inside Easter eggs. They were laughing, and the balcony of my parents' house was tangled in threads black as gunpowder. It was terrifying. The couples settled in my childhood home, and we watched them through the window. For they were wicked. There were black threads all the way to the dining-room tablecloth, and my brothers were dismantling Lebel rifle cartridges. Ever since then, the police have had me under watch.

1914

A corset barely contains his jutting belly. His plumed helmet has been flattened; his face is a terrifying death mask, but dark and so ferocious you'd think you were looking at the horn of a rhinoceros or an extra tooth for his terrible jawbone. Oh, ominous vision of German death.

War

At night, the outer boulevards are full of snow. The thieves are soldiers; they ambush me with laughter and swords; they take everything I have. I escape only to fall down in another square. Is it the courtyard of a barracks or an inn? So many swords! So many lancers! It's snowing! They inject me with a syringe: a poison to murder me. A skull veiled in black bites my finger. Ripples from streetlamps cast the light of my death onto the snow.

Grave News! New Graves!

At a performance of *For the Crown* at the Opera House, when Desdemona sings "My father's in Goritz but my heart's in Paris," a shot rang out from a box on the fifth balcony, and then another from the stands, and straightaway rope ladders were unrolled. A man tried to slide down from the beams: a bullet stopped him at the balcony. All the spectators were armed, and it turned out that the auditorium was full of nothing but . . . and . . . Then there was the murder of the person in the next seat, petrol bombs bursting into flame. There were battles for balcony seats, the stage seat, and the folding seats of the stalls, and it all lasted for eighteen days. Perhaps the two camps were kept supplied—I don't know for sure, but what I do know is that the journalists couldn't wait to see such an awful spectacle, that one of them, being ill, sent her Ladyship, his mother, in his place, and that she was excited by the cold-blooded courage of a young French gentleman who held out for eighteen days in the wings without any sustenance save for a little broth. This episode from the Balcony War has done a lot for the recruitment of volunteers from the provinces. And sitting on my riverbank under my trees, I know of three brothers in brand-new uniforms who embraced one another dry-eyed, while their families searched in their attic wardrobes for knitted sweaters.

To write to the *Figaro* that I stole a rifle! The wretch! It's him, the hotel owner. My brother forgot his rifle at the Paris hotel. The owner got hold of it and he's writing to the *Figaro* to tell them it was me. It's not difficult to put right. You address a letter to "The Gentleman in the Orchestra," c/o "Theater News." Would that be any use? I'm leaving the hotel: the bed is never made, old chambermaids come into my room to mock me in my misery; the young maids only know how to bare their shoulders. Have I ever stolen a rifle?

The hotel again! My friend Paul has been taken prisoner by the Germans. My God, where is he? Lautenbourg, a lodging house on rue Saint-Sulpice, but I don't know his room number. The hotel desk is a pulpit that is too high for me to see over. I'd like . . . isn't there a Mademoiselle Cypriani here . . . it must be room 21 or 26 or 28, and now here I am dreaming of the cabbalistic meaning of these numbers. It's Paul the Germans have arrested for betraying his colonel: what kind of times are we living in? 21, 26, 28 are the figures painted in white on a black background with three keys. But who is Mademoiselle Cypriani? Yet another spy.

Not My Kind of Poem

for you, Rimbaud

My horse has tripped on the semiquavers. The notes spatter all the way up to the green heaven of my soul: the eighth heaven.

Apollo was a doctor, and I'm a pianist at heart, if not in reality. With the flat notes and sets of bars, one would have to unload sketched steamers and collect the tiny flags in order to compose canticles.

The tiny is enormous. The one who conceived of Napoleon as an insect between two branches of a tree, who painted his nose too big in watercolor, and who depicted his court in such soft colors, was he not greater than Napoleon himself, oh Ataman Prajapati!

The tiny one, that's the note.

A man will have photos of his ancestors on him just as God did Napoleon, oh Spinoza! My ancestors and I are notes on a harp. God conceived Saint Helena and the sea between two branches of a tree. My black horse has good eyes, albeit albino, but he's tripped on a harp's notes.

Maxims and drawings sent by the patron of a house of ill repute in Hanoi to the *Assiette au Beurre*, a comic or political magazine in Paris that had some success around 1900. The Hanoi drawings aimed to emulate the modernism of M. d'O . . . ; but they were more worthy of the Guimet Museum. While we cannot demonstrate here the plasticity of this work, we can show you its moral dimensions, which will be the envy of the world.

"An old man does not say, I love you; he says, love me."

"An old man no longer has vices; it is the vices which have him."

"One does not have a passion for tea; nevertheless, one has to drink it. Some women are like tea."

"The fiftieth night of love! I shall be obliged to escort you back to the house you came from if you don't stop asking for so much."

"In a tent on a beach, we found the corpse of an old man. He'd killed himself after a gambling loss. He could no longer afford the upkeep of another old man's two wives plus the old man himself."

"With women, be fatherly but firm."

The drawing that reinforced this last maxim depicted a man dressed like the poet B raising a truncheon over a woman with messy hair.

The patron of the house of ill repute in Hanoi has been searching for his work in the illustrated magazines for fifteen years. The *Assiette au Beurre* no longer appears, but he reckons the bottom of this Butter Dish lies on a table somewhere. This impromptu author, who has been a white slave trader and a black slave trader, a spy, a convict, a croupier, a diplomatic agent, and an entrepreneur in the funeral business, is an experienced man. He is not the only one whose experience surprises us with its poverty.

Everything takes place as it did in the time of Alfred de Musset. Here I am in a furnished lodging on rue du Rempart. A composer is reproaching me, by candlelight, for not having gone to listen to his ballet at the Opera: then, on an old grand piano, I try to hold some long notes while he performs some vocal variations . . . and in the alcove is a woman, but this woman is his ill mother.

Here I am at the ball. There's lots of gossip: "Look how she's dressed! A red turban, and her daughter's wearing one, too! She's in love, ladies, she's in love. The worthy Madame de Pont-Aven is in love. All those turbans! Those changes of hairstyle! She hangs around the salons all night because he's there!" When I went inside, two women wanted to know which of them I liked best, and I liked them both. A fine gentleman showed us how to dance the English Chain and the lesson went on and on. While the English Chain was being organized, the gas lamp (did we have a gas lamp?) was turned down and then the flame was increased as the music grew louder, thanks to a technical innovation as bold as it was ingenious. When the Chain got going, the piano went brilliantly and the gas lamp too. What an innovation! Now I was by the fireplace. The lady of the house had flowers sent to me because I was ill. These baskets of flowers made me laugh and cry at the same time. The salon was filling with turbans and bare shoulders: all these people looked like bit players from the French Theater. Two ladies were saying: "In our world we are not to be taken for fools, and we don't take anyone else for a fool, either!" Two gentlemen tried to remember a riddle made up of two lines of verse, then went outside to duel. A great deal was made of my joys, my tears, my flowers by the fireplace.

Not My Kind of Poem

for you, Baudelaire

Near a holly bush through whose leaves a city could be seen, Don Juan, Rothschild, Faust, and a painter were having a chat.

"I amassed a great fortune," said Rothschild, "but since it left me discontent, I amassed more and more, hoping to recover the joy my first million brought me."

"I kept looking for love in the midst of all my troubles," said Don Juan. "To be loved and yet not to love is torture, but I went on searching in the hope of finding once again the passion of my first love."

"When I found the secret that brought me glory," said the painter, "I looked for other secrets to fill my mind; because of that, I was denied my previous fame, and I've gone back to my old formula though it now disgusts me."

"I quit science for happiness," said Faust, "but now I've returned to science, even though my methods are old-fashioned, because there is no happiness except in the search."

Beside them was a young woman, crowned with artificial ivy who said, "I'm bored, I'm too beautiful."

And God from behind the holly bush:

"I know the universe, and I'm bored."

Declamatory Poem

It's neither the horror of the white dusk nor the pallid dawn which the moon refuses to illuminate, but rather the sad light of dreams where you float with glitter in your hair, you Republics, Defeats, Triumphs! What are these Fates? What are these Furies? Is this France in a Phrygian cap? Is it you, England? Is it Europe? Is it the world on the Bull-Cloud of Minos? There's a great stillness in the air and Napoleon is listening to the music of the silence on the plains of Waterloo. Oh Moon, may your horns protect him! There's a tear on his pale cheeks. The procession of ghosts is fascinating. "Hail to you! Hail! Our horses' manes are wet with dew, we are the cuirassiers! Our helmets shine like the stars and in the shadows our dusty battalions are like the divine hand of destiny. Napoleon! Napoleon! We are born and we die." "Charge! Charge! Ghosts, I order you to charge!" The light snickers: the cuirassiers salute with their swords and snicker. They're no longer flesh and blood. And thus, Napoleon listens to the music of silence and repents, for where are the forces that God had given him? But here comes the sound of a drum! A child is beating the drum: on his high bearskin cap, there's a red flag, and this child really is alive: this is France! Now around the plains of Waterloo, in the sad light of dreams where you float, glitter in your hair, Republics, Defeats, Triumphs, the horror of the white dusk is no longer here, nor the pallid dawn which the moon refuses to illuminate.

"What do you want from me?" says Mercury.

 "Your smile and your teeth," says Venus.

 "They're false. What is it that you want from me?"

 "Your messenger's staff."

 "It must stay with me always."

 "Bring it over here, you divine mailman."

 You have to read that in the original Greek: it's called an Idyll. At school, a friend of mine who kept failing his exams said to me: "If you translated one of Daudet's novels into Greek, you'd be properly prepared for the exam. But I can't work at night. It makes my mother cry!" You have to read that in the Greek, too, gentlemen: it's an idyll, or ειδυλλος, a small scene.

Poem

Rub out the heads of the Empire's generals! But they're still alive! All I can do is change their hats: the hats are full of explosives and these gentlemen of the Empire don't mess around: guncotton explodes. I had no idea guncotton was such a white dove. Let's go into this biblical landscape! But it's a woodcut: a row of uneven houses, a sandbank behind a trickle of water, a trickle of water behind a palm tree. It's an illustration for *Saint Matorel*, the novel by Max Jacob. This is where we go for a walk, Mlle Leonie and I; but I didn't know we were carrying suitcases in this book. The generals sitting at this banquet with their hats on were alive, but does that mean Mlle Leonie and I are not? I can't enter this biblical landscape; it's a woodcut: I even know the engraver. When the hats of the Empire's generals were put back on their heads, everything returned to how it was; I reentered the woodcut and peace reigned in the desert of art.

Anecdote

A carpenter commended one of his debtors. This was reported to the person in question, who grew anxious and rushed off in search of friends.

"Where are you going? Your creditor reveres you."

"What? Can't you see that if he starts praising me, it's because he's sure he'll get his money back? And if he's sure of delivering me from debt, it's because he'll send in the bailiffs. I'm calling on friends to find a creditor who won't be as hard on me as he is, someone who'll pay him off."

As I told this story to an artist, I described the carpenter's family: the wife with uncorseted breasts, the hands rocking their child to sleep, the young worker's beard.

"My dear friend," the artist said to me, "if you give the carpenter a beard, don't foist a child onto him as well, I beg you. If the father is clean-shaven, then the picture won't be so silly, and the anecdote will work better."

And since I didn't understand, the artist shrugged his shoulders. I shrugged my shoulders, too, for reasons I won't get into.

Poem

When our ship reached the Indian Ocean islands, we realized
we had no maps. We had to disembark! It was then we discov-
ered who was on board: that bloodthirsty man who gives his
wife tobacco, only to snatch it back. The islands were scattered
everywhere. On the clifftop, we could make out some small
Negroes in bowler hats. "Maybe they'll have some maps." We
took the cliff path: it was a rope ladder; perhaps along the lad-
der there would be some maps, maybe even Japanese maps.
We kept going up. Finally, when there were no more rungs
(but ivory crabs in some places), we had to climb using our
wrists. My African brother acquitted himself very well, while
I discovered some rungs where there hadn't been any. Having
reached the top, we're on a wall. My brother leaps off. Me, I'm
at the window. I could never make up my mind to jump: it's a
wall made of red boards. "Take a tour around it," my African
brother cries. There are no more steps, nor passengers, nor
boat, nor small Negroes; there's the tour still to be taken. But
what tour? It's disheartening.

"I'll be returning to your house, Lady, every morning, until your son the captain returns from the colonies."

"It'd be a lot easier to consult the yearbook to find out what day he's here, if you want to see him that badly."

We entered the lady's house when she wasn't there. My sister declared that she had lovely furniture: a bed inlaid with ivory which had come loose.

"One sees these beds everywhere. Anyway, it isn't beautiful since it isn't ancient, and it isn't ancient since here, inlaid, is a portrait of the lady's son."

"Don't use the lady's nail file. First, because you don't know how to use a nail file when it's made of ivory, and also because using a lady's nail file when she isn't present is not the sort of thing one does. If she comes in, what will she say? If she says nothing, what will she be thinking?"

"I'll say that I'm waiting for her son, the captain, who has gone to the colonies."

"She'll find out that you've been abusing her hospitality, and she'll chase you out, and you'll have to go back to drinking all by yourself on café terraces."

Poem

He's grown taller, he's grown fatter, he's kept that look we used to see in the mirror. "Three heads under one cap," we said. He can't stand hernia supports. The maid doesn't want to bring a lamp, we'll grab some candles. As for me, I no longer have the contacts to find a position again. Filling in forms! Formulas! There's a constant factor of 2,241, by which one has to multiply the others: I'll go to the druggist and consult his huge dictionary. "Sir, it's question of *Kieros o phaos*! Pierre's exhausted.—We'll look things up together." He was the son of a certain A. On the way back, I'll pass by the laundress, the one who gives me stockings instead of my socks, stockings with a thousand holes.

Poem

Hail on the sea; night's descending. "Light the cattle beacon!"

The old courtesan has died in the inn: there's nothing but laughter in the house.

It's hailing and they're showing some films in the schoolhouse for the sailors.

The teacher has a beautiful face. Here I am in the country. There are two men watching the cattle beacon shine.

"At last, you're here!" the teacher says to me. "Are you going to take notes during the films? The little band of assistants will give their table over to you."

"Notes? What should I be taking notes on? The subjects of the films?"

"No! You will condense the rhythm of the projector with that of the hail, and also the laughter of those present at the death of the old courtesan, to have an idea of what Purgatory is like."

Poem

This was the pedagogical examination room. Some men and women were sitting round a table.

"Are you taking the exam, Monsieur Max?"

"I haven't registered."

And I went into the next room to sit down, musing over the subject of the examination, which was this so-called aphorism by a so-called philosopher:

"How do you treat chickens that fly over a somber background in a lively fashion?"

I was passing the time alone, waiting for a friend, remembering a clifftop trip by carriage with my father the evening before, and thinking about the essay I would be writing if I had registered. I was also considering the question of modern dictation versus scholarly dictation. I had texts in front of me in every language. When I went back into the room, the candidates were reunited and putting their heads together to come up with a model answer. They divided the subject up into paragraphs, and they were actually talking about chickens with a great deal of erudition regarding the subject of farmyards and with an inkling of something else. They asked me for my opinion. I said that it seemed to me that what was wanted was an essay on the special education required for the children of Paris.

In a place in Algiers which brings to mind Constantinople, gold epaulettes were no more than acacia branches, or the other way around. The latest fashion is for women to bedeck themselves everywhere with bunches of celluloid grapes as jewels. A horse ate the earrings off one of my beautiful friends and died, the carmine of its muzzle and the fuchsia of the vine juice making up a lethal poison.

The Tree Rodents

Solitary, or imprisoned, or working, Alexander Dumas père consoled himself with the smell of a woman's clothes. Three identical men—same round hat, same small size—came across one another and were astonished to find they all looked so alike, and each of them came up with the same idea: to steal the consolation of the lonely.

I thought he was ruined, but he still has some slaves and a lot of coins around the house. The sopranos in their swimsuits on the rocks are half nude. In the evening, we climbed aboard the carriages and the small trains glided beneath the pines. I thought he was ruined! ... He's even found me a publisher! The publisher's given me a tortoise with a varnished, pink shell. Even a ducatoon would be of more help.

Are you going out? They'll see how sick you are: the lanterns on wheels are watching you and the rocking zebra ends up making you lightheaded.

◊

I declare myself worldwide, oviparous, giraffe, thirsty, Sinophobic, and hemispherical. I drink from the springs of the atmosphere, and it laughs concentrically and farts at my uncertainty.

◊

And when the Polish lancer's limbs were chopped off, his bottle smashed, the only thing left to him was an eye, the eye which sang "The Two Grenadiers."

◊

What are you missing, oh skull, to look like a chicken's ass? A bladder? And to look like an ostrich? Goose flesh.

◊

Wearing a fool's cap, the knife grinder (he's death) parts a folded cape of cherry-colored silk to sharpen a great sword. A butterfly on the wheel stops him.

◊

His white arms became my whole horizon.

◊

A fire's blaze is a rose on the peacock's opened tail.

◊

The game of dominoes on the tablecloth made us think of death and the maid's white apron was unable to banish this idea.

◊

I dreamt that nuns put down flowerbeds in the Sacré-Coeur, for God loves the earth, and that they scattered them with confetti, for God loves joy.

◊

Portrait of grandpa by a child of five: a bull's head smoking a pipe. The family's delighted; grandpa incensed.

◊

It was two in the morning: the three old ladies were so elegant, dressed as they would have been fifty years ago: black lace shawls, bonnets with ribbon ties, cameos, black silk dresses showing off the fabric's pleats. The sidewalk was deserted, and their eyes, full of tears, rose toward a window, through whose curtain a light shone faintly.

◊

If you put your ear to the tick-tock of your ear, you'll properly hear something inside you which isn't really you, but a demon or the devil.

◊

When one paints a picture, it changes entirely with each touch. It turns like a cylinder and is almost endless. When it stops turning, the picture is done. My last one depicted the Tower of Babel by candlelight.

◊

At the tobacconists in Belgium, the pipes are mounted in fan-like displays that reach all the way up to the ceiling. A Belgian child told me that's what the wings of the devil are like.

◊

Augustine was a farm girl when the President spotted her. To avoid a scandal, he awarded her some titles and some teaching diplomas, then added a "de" to her name, some money, and the more he provided for her, the worthier she was of him. As for me, a poor Breton peasant, I have given myself everything: the title of duke, the right to wear a monocle. I've grown in stature and made my thoughts greater, and I'll never be worthy of myself.

◊

Huge fruits on a dwarf tree, much too big for it. A palace on the rocks of an island too small for it. Art in a nation far too fine for it.

◊

A horse has escaped from the institute's stables. The foal has come to a stop near the bridge. Napoleon I chases after it. The valet, a marshal, if you please, catches up with the Emperor, who's forgotten his little cape and his bottle of Rome, or is that rum?

◊

A dancing bear left the village square and went to piss against a wall.

◊

It so happens that when you snore, the material world wakes the other one.

◊

Coming down rue de Rennes, I bit into my bread with such feeling that it felt like I was tearing into my own heart.

◊

A pale blue thorn bush in the light of the moon is a belltower.

◊

In the Andean Cordilleras, the grapes growing on the hops can't be seen.

◊

The chains shed light, but the hosts which are apples do not: it's a chandelier.

◊

There's nothing left but the tops of the trees, there's nothing left but the top of a house roof, there's nothing left but a hurting buttock, telling a lie to uncover the truth and see who's right.

◊

To show the importance of dinner service to the Rothschilds, a magazine showed the family at the bottom of an enormous pile of plates. A reader is examining the ants with a magnifying glass: "Which one's Henry? Which one's Henry?"

◊

During a journey in Algeria, the emperor Napoleon III, with the empress, his Egeria, had to save himself by going through the mangroves in full dress. What made matters worse was that the emperor was wearing Wellingtons which hurt his feet.

◊

The infant, the *ifant*, the elephant, the frog, and the sautéed apple.

◊

The periscope of Mentana is an underground grotto, its rock frame an elegant rectangle. The lake is of Indian ink and fits the frame; two black-faced seraphim bang heads at a cross-angle, left and right; at the edge, at the foot of the rocky column, and on a step, a smaller-than-life bureaucrat in morning coat scratches his bald crown. It puts me in mind of a shop window, this periscope of Mentana.

◊

The left-handed, hunchbacked bird called Morguë will not make its nest with anything other than ears of wheat and decorates it with nasturtiums around the edges as an afterthought.

◊

Hallelujah
Under the thujas
the Prince of Lusignan
screwed his woman
It smelt of naphthalene
They hadn't left the harbor
And the stink's stayed there

◊

They've got some armchairs on mechanical rollers so they can roll over the skies, heads down.

◊

The lace threads on N.S.'s breast carried away by a sparrow.

◊

They make hay at the Armenonville pavilion.

◊

In these Breton woods where the carriage goes, there's only one mocking angel: the peasant woman in red in the branches who laughs at my ignorance of the Celtic language.

◊

To take their revenge on the author who gave them life, the heroes he created have hidden his penholder.

◊

Around the bay, to the north, to the south, behind every rock lives a brother or sister of Napoleon.

◊

The horizon's boiling. Sun! Take all these white and pink hammocks! You won't get mine: it's amber and embroidered with jet—on this side, at least.

Title: *DESCRIPTION OF AN AVENUE*

◊

The screw, with its spiral climbing around it, which finds fulfillment at its point: screwing.

◊

The white rocks in a heap and the climber of these clouds, the airship.

◊

The archangel struck by lightning only just had time to undo his tie. It looked like he was still praying.

◊

Mist, fogweb.

◊

Dawn on the horizon is a tin mirror casting its reflection on a house.

◊

It was a Pierrot costume in percale with breeches too short to even reach the knee and which I rented, haggling with a certain sergeant. I've found some letters in them! Yes! Letters I shall publish when the boutique is demolished, or the sergeant is dead.

◊

Play tennis, escalator steps. The ball stays too long in the air, quivering, and falls back onto the moving belly of the escalator, or the accordion.

◊

The mosaic of paving stones simulates a bas-relief to make me completely lose my balance. Oh, the malice of architects!

◊

At the foot of the bed, in the wardrobe mirror, we see our two sinful heads, guillotined.

◊

The waterspouts on the Seine shot as high as the towers! I'm lost in the maze of a floodgate and bridge.

◊

You've got it wrong, my good angel. Why these consoling words? I was crying with joy.

◊

The splash made by that ink gushing from its bottle! It's not a frog, but a tiny orchestra conductor, who's pointing at the footlights and the hem of a white dress.

◊

Do they believe then that we have truffles in our hearts?

◊

Skip down the staircase—your feet won't touch it.

◊

Principles come unstuck: the proletariat is circumspect.

◊

So many people who love me are waiting on the ship's deck, but how do I get on board?

◊

Lines of bricks, library!

◊

Between the curtains, the beam is a slipway for the smoke! No! For the dancing blue angels!

◊

The artillery of the Sacré-Coeur or the canonization of Paris.

◊

The honeycombs of an endless silk curtain are how I imagine the houses in New York.

◊

The sun is made of lace.

◊

A corner of pale blue lining, a corner of fur like a fold of sky over a corner of the Pole.

◊

There is so much tangled coral that water can't be far away: it's this hair and water, it's this topaz earring.

◊

The Zouave who'd watched the century pass spoke thus with a regretful tone: "In Algeria, we would go out in our carriages and gaze at our moustaches in pocket mirrors, but if we took out cigarette papers it was likely they were spotted with blood."

◊

The flame of his hand wants to reunite with his profile. His body is the back of a chair, his knees the feet of his paltry throne. His scepter, which another harlequin knocks with his motionless flute while dancing, rests casually on his shoulder.

◊

Like a ship is the ancient poet
as well as a dahlia, the layered poem
Dahlia! Dahlia Delilah ties!

◊

The world has a crocodile for a spine, its royal headband is a railway line. It has minarets for teeth and its handkerchief is one of the dresses of Thaïs folded into twenty squares.

◊

When my brother came back from his voyage, he embraced me. "What are you reading?" he asked me. "Or rather, how old are you? For a book gives away one's age." It was *The Carapassionate Pilgrim* by the author of *The Scottish Pilgrim Girl*.[3]

◊

It's a street corner. The priests rush to it like wine into a funnel. They've got headbands to keep their hats in place and hands to hold onto the headbands. They've all got toothache.

◊

I saw my old teacher of rhetoric again and with a woman. It was only their heads I saw, joylessly eating chocolate eclairs. The big, bored head and the small, bossy head. Ah, the revenge of humanity on the humanities. But I kept from laughing at them to get my own back: that's the revenge of the humanities on humanity.

◊

Like reeds leaning over a pool, the rain falls into the hollows of mountains where the valley flattens out. Waterfalls are not far away.

◊

The cast-iron plate blackened by smoke depicts a branch, and beneath the branch, a man and woman riding horses. A manservant waits for them on a mound. It's a stove door. On the other door, the same scene, but the man has fallen off his horse and the manservant is far away.

◊

Before dawn, a dog barks, then the angels begin to whisper.

◊

Sanderini was up for a good time. He was entertaining the Prince of Schönbrunn on a desert island: "Is that a fire on the shore?" No, those are the sails of frigates rounding the rocks of Stymphale. It was as if a lifebelt had raised them over the island's head.

◊

Mountains, you are like frothy milk soup under the airship, and from beyond, as if from a gigantic dice cup, the gentlemanly globe appears, the forehead of Father Double Sphere.

◊

There are more white ones than black. Why do they leap about like sand fleas? Would it be because the chorus is made up of *Montagnards* or because their leaps keep time with the way the song is sung?

◊

This smoke which chases itself over the curves of the blue silk curtains decorated with deep red roses in velvet, this smoke is the cat which passes by.

◊

On a photo, someone's painted Victor Hugo's eyelids red. It gives him a bloodthirsty look. He's holding what seems to be a green silk scarf.

◊

The rescuer on the canal is announced by swollen water and by the height of the vessel. The rest is just a bit of greenery on the glory.

◊

The ballet leads us back to reality: victorias with scarlet wheels, the canons of war, the crowd, but above all the sky! The sky! A real sky! Reality leads us back to the ballet.

◊

The roof is four, four, four: there are four of them. The step is a lawn on which we work, and which makes them jealous. The roofs are amaranthine: a reflection of a raging storm! Rage! Rage! And the whole is made of sugar, of stucco, a beehive, rich and ugly.

◊

If only, says the wind, I could play marbles with the trees, the way I do with the clouds and the rest. Now, in his impotent fury, he shakes their thick green canopy, ends up tearing into it and hurling what he's so dreadfully ripped away into the river.

◊

In his sack, the mailman of avenue de l'Opéra has a bird as plump as the pearls which line the sack's black velvet. He treats it to a drink on the café terraces.

◊

In the morning, at the foot of the mountain, voices echo as in a corridor.

◊

> Sometimes a swimming fish
> Shows its white belly in the waves;
> The airship, a flying fish,
> May offer its whiteness to the cloud;

The dancer, as she turns
On stage, shows every tier
A back swimming with diamonds.

◊

Oh, the silky bivalves! We've seen a tapestry of them: it was like a peacock's feathers in that place where the egg comes from, but phosphorescent in the diamond of its white ivory, and its violet was paler, too.

◊

The brazier, zero. It's furious at not being a triangle equipped with black wings. It chews its own tail. It's crisscrossed by blue rails which rally, raze, and rail at it.

◊

A thousand bouquets of little forests, a thousand little forests of bouquets and a thousand chamomiles. If you want, my sweet, you may wear your mantilla. The pool at night has vertebrae as deeply green as the mosses of my pistils.

◊

Don't light it. Don't light the lamp. The abbot would learn my secret; he'd follow me into this room, and my father himself would come in. It's like a knife at the door to my heart.

◊

The mystery is in this life, reality is in the other; if you love me, if you love me, I'll help you see reality.

◊

Isn't it true that the ear of wheat and the poplar tree bear some resemblance? One signifies abundance, the other pride.

◊

My Selene, mine own, is not an enormous lump of petroleum jelly with, oh Selene, hair tangled all around some large-toothed comb; she's yellow-striped onyx that burns and burnishes.

◊

The man in the white smock was pulling the cow by the nostrils between sky and mountain. The implacable smell of burnt cow grows fainter and fainter. The woman's breast is not for sale for it hadn't been the cow he was pulling by the nostrils. She was mooing.

◊

When the Good Lord breathes down on us, it makes a luminous triangle that flattens the clouds against the rooftops and fields; when He breathes on high, it makes a rainbow.

◊

Don't you find that models in fashion magazines can come to life?

◊

A cave whose terrible sloping roofs threaten the sand. Now, an electric ray of light from the stalactites of a café under the arcade transforms a bundle of seaweed into a loaf of precious stones: we turn a corner.

◊

A patch of blue sky, a bit of smoke like swan's down: angels on a journey.

◊

A diadem is transformed into a thousand legislators' heads.

◊

Because of the number of dead people there, I imagine Heaven as Paris this third Thursday of Lent, and Hell as a panic-stricken crowd of families in a port when a storm arrives.

◊

It's a branch with three flowers: the branch is the color of snow, and the flowers too: the flowers hang their heads, the branches too. Everything is pearly and nothing is held in place. Yes, it is! It's attached to a headband, at the front, white and smiling.

◊

Nothing but the son of an ancient librarian on a dark stairwell. Nothing. Nothing but the story of a ball no one will be going to. They bring my brother in on a bed that is eaten away by insects: "I'm going to die and you're not going to the ball!" The question is settled. So, I'll dress all in black and it won't be for the ball.

◊

Seen against the light or otherwise, I don't exist, and yet I am a tree.

◊

Water insects fly toward the silver lizard, which serves as a fountain mouth, and then toward the gray stiches of skirts.

◊

When a piece of clothing is given to a magician, he can reveal who wears it. As for me, when I put on my shirt, I know what I was thinking the day before.

◊

Its flowers are like forget-me-nots, and they're arranged in such a fashion that one would think the bush is a clown who, with one foot behind him, holds out his two arms like a candelabra.

◊

M. de Max offered all his profiles to each of the two parties like so many giant prisms.

◊

Some sugar lozenges, a blue half-moon, another white one: the soupy-colored atmosphere is saturated with them; every head in the crowd on the boulevards has a halo this third Thursday of Lent. Automobiles shoot through like cannons.

◊

Wherever at night there's an ivory tray, there's phosphorescence: that's the lamps.

◊

One would never think there were men sleeping there if it weren't for the black ties they're wearing.

◊

In houses, the stains on the ceiling are signs of the lives of their inhabitants: here are two bears reading a newspaper by the fire.

◊

The top of the Pont des Saints-Pères was warm this morning, even though the Seine was frozen; it occurred to me that perhaps braziers were lit in the evening under the bridges for the homeless and that it was this which kept the heat there.

◊

Why do you keep your parasol open, madame, in your friend's bathroom? It's just while the old woman cuts her corns, it's to protect her from the sun behind the white marble bathtub.

◊

That German was crazy about art, silk scarves, and fattened hens. In his country, the Reine Claude plum is painted on the scarves; at mealtimes, we also know who loiters around the fattened hens.

◊

I'll bring you my two sons said the old acrobat to the Virgin of the Rocks, who was playing a mandolin. The youngest knelt in his pretty little costume; the other came forward with a fish at the end a stick.

Frontispiece

Yes, it fell from the nipple of my breast without me realizing it. As a ship with its crew emerges from the shelter of the rocks without increasing the sea's trembling, without the earth sensing this new adventure, a new poem fell from my Cybele breast, and without me even noticing.

Moon Poem

There are three mushrooms in the night which are the moon. As abruptly as the cuckoo in the clock starts singing, they change position each month at midnight. There are rare flowers in the garden which are tiny sleeping men, who are the reflections in a mirror. There's a luminous incense holder loitering in my dark room, and then two ... phosphorescent airships, the reflections in a mirror. Inside my head there's a bee speaking.

M. René Ghil's Java Poem Called the Ksours ▬▬▬

With the swipe of a fingernail, they enter the fold of their eyelids to give their eyes the stare of statues. No one has the right to sleep here anymore. Those women who have eyes like their coffee-colored stags . . . Oh, your tiara, coral phallus, Tao-Phen-Tsu! . . . They'll never be forgotten. Three dwarves, naval officers, climbed down the champagne-colored cliffs to dance the *boulalaïka* with the concubines of Champagne, and that night, two music-school students left their . . . (here some wild behavior, but not unbecoming) to play a duet on painted kazoos in the yard under the electric-lit . . . With the swipe of a fingernail, they enter the fold of their eyelids to give their eyes the stare of statues, but those who have eyes like sugar virgins will never let anyone touch them there. They sing the language of the cicadas, and the god-princes eat slices of bread and butter with the tips of their fingers.

Something horribly cold falls onto my shoulders. Something gluey attaches itself to my neck. A voice from the sky is crying, "Monster!" without me knowing if it's talking about me and my vices or the sticky creature that's attached itself to me.

"You can't swim twice in the same river," said Heraclitus the philosopher. Nonetheless, it's always the same people who sail back up again. Happy or sad, they pass by at the same time each day. I've named you all, passersby on rue Ravignan, after the famous dead of history. Here's Agamemnon! Here's Madame Hanska! Ulysses is a milkman! Patroclus is at the end of the street while a pharaoh is right beside me. Castor and Pollux are the ladies on the sixth floor. But you, old ragpicker, you, who in the magic of morning, while I'm turning off my lovely big lamp, have come to pick over still-living cast-offs, you whom I don't know, mysterious poor ragpicker, you, ragpicker, I've given you a celebrated and noble name. I've named you Dostoevsky.

The Inconvenience of Cuttings

The head was nothing more than a little white ball in the great white bed. The puce silk eiderdown was by the lamp with its seams suitably braided with trimmings. The mother in this white valley, her teeth taken out, was at the heart of great things; and her son by the bedside table with his seventeen years and his face hair which his pimples stopped him from shaving was amazed that from this big old bed, from this hollow valley of a bed, from this little toothless ball could emanate such a marvelous winning personality, just as brilliant as his. However, the little old ball didn't want him to leave behind the lamp by the white valley. It would have been better for him if he hadn't left, for this lamp has always impeded him from living anywhere else, now that he's no longer near her.

Christmas Story

for Madame Sylvette Olin

There was once an architect or a horse: it was a horse rather than an architect, in Philadelphia, who was asked: "Do you know Cologne Cathedral? Then get a cathedral built the same as the one in Cologne." And, since he didn't know Cologne Cathedral, they put him in prison. But an angel appeared to him in prison and said: "Wolfrang! Wolfrang! Why do you despair?" "I have to stay in prison because I don't know Cologne Cathedral!" "What you're missing is Rhine wine to build Cologne Cathedral, but show them the design and they'll let you out." And the angel gave him the design, and he showed them the design, and so he was released from prison, but he couldn't build the cathedral because he wasn't able to find the Rhine wine. He had the idea of having the Rhine wine delivered to him in Philadelphia, but they sent him some awful French wine from the Moselle, with the result that he wasn't able to build Cologne Cathedral in Philadelphia: all he made was a dreadful Protestant church.

Translated from German or Bosnian ▬▬▬

For Madame Édouard Fillacier

My horse has stopped. Stop yours too, friend—I'm afraid. Between us and the slopes of the hill, the grassy slopes of the hill, there's a woman, unless it's a great cloud. Stop! She's calling me. She's calling me and I see her beating heart. Her arm makes a sign for me to follow, her arm . . . unless her arm's a cloud.

"Stop, friend, I'm afraid, stop! Between the trees of the hill, the trees at an angle on the hill, I've seen an eye, unless that eye is a cloud. It stares at me, making me nervous. Stop! It's following in our footsteps along the road, unless that eye's a cloud."

"Listen, friend. Ghosts of this life or another, let's not speak of them in the city or they'll treat us as troublemakers."

Let's Celebrate Death

"I'm offering you free seats! So that'll be two francs fifty." It's for a party at the Trocadéro to celebrate the death of a famous Russian author, who's on his way to glory. They hand out booklets, one of which is made of wood carved in a childlike manner, the other with color illustrations. The death of the Russian is represented by a striking purple smock, while Maroussia and Anna lean over him in their great national costume: pigtails and tiara. In one image, the young girls, who have to attend the funeral, appear to be held on a burning staircase under the pretext of giving them a tear-stained complexion to show they've cried. There weren't even three people in the Trocadéro amphitheater. It was left to the organizers to wear the tear-stained complexion.

The Novel

There's only ever been one cozy little ground floor for me. It's in Quimper and has two little windows which open under a small balcony. Coming back from high school, our eyes were always on them. One day, to take revenge for some trick, someone threw ink out of the window onto my overcoat. What spite there was in those purple stains! I grabbed the guilty wrist and pulled. Out came the hip of a woman in a dressing gown. That woman would one day be mine.

Double Life

The castle has two pointed towers, and we stretch out on the bosom of a hillock just opposite. The old maid has the appearance of a high altar; the castle steps have the appearance of a high altar, and here it is, supported by doves, flying toward us. Now this high altar was dropping some brochures: Charity Sale. And the old maid offered me one without realizing I had more of a right to be sold than to be selling, to be bought than to be buying, to be the beneficiary rather than the benefactor.

"Guess what time it is! You'll never guess what time it is."

"I saw magic shadows on my wall tonight. I notice that the lime which makes the tiles shine is scratched, and I imagine the neighbor's lamp created those fantastical projected images which make me all the more afraid because they're always the same."

"Ah, you're enjoying yourself here! You'll be sorry to go to Paris for a few days to enroll at the Faculty of Law. Guess what time it is!"

"Ten past one."

"Your watch is fast. It's half past twelve. Well, you'll have a good time with your friends. There are quite a few friends in your neighborhood you can get together with for a picnic."

"I'd rather have a formal invitation to a proper meal."

"You'd prefer nicking food to picnicking."

"Look at this bedside rug: it depicts a garland! It's made of rubber: I'll make a raincoat out of it for when the insults come pouring down."

"Dreadful!" my mother interjected. "Dreadful tendencies in this boy toward parasitism, I mean paralysis."

A Bit of Art Criticism

Jacques Claes is truly a Dutch painter's name. Let us cast an eye, if you will, on his origins. Little Jacques's mother put vinegar on her face to make it look pale, as she herself confessed, which explains why the maestro's pictures seem varnished. In Jacques's village, on Saint Roofer's Day, it was the custom for roofers to let themselves fall from rooftops without crushing passersby. They also had to throw ropes up from the sidewalk to the chimneys. Altogether very picturesque, and this surely must have given our painter his picturesque style.

L'eglisiglia del Amore, l'odore del Tarquino, in short, all the monuments of Rome on a *bouteglia* of wine and the corresponding register to prove we've drunk copiously, but will abstain: guzzling from the bottle's neck, to make a bottleneck in our race for the taste of water. If we're going to repent, we may as well abstain. The fickle rainbow is nothing more than a volcanic decoration on the corner of the label. Mum's the word! And let's compare one liter with another: *el spatio del Baccio* and the *Bacco nel cor.*[4]

M. Le Président of the Republic Visits the Horticultural Exhibition

Tall palm trees so gracious you'd think we were in Algeria, as much from their attitude as their altitude. Tall palm trees! They were only or will only be made of plaster, alas! There's a huge head here below like the ogre's in *Tom Thumb*! Is he asleep? No, he's smiling, and his hand hiding the sky, the enormous sky of Algeria, his hand soaring over to make us think it's night, brushes over thick foliage with a light touch and returns with a bit of dust on the index finger. Aha, our lady the cleaning woman? Aha! The scene is changing; now the dahlias are giants: red and white, arranged as if for a chromolithograph, and Monsieur le Président Tom Thumb is now wealthy enough to relieve his woodcutter parents of the palm trees.

How Confession Works

On the road leading to the racetrack, there was a beggar who looked like a servant. "Have pity," he used to say, "I'm sick, I'll gamble away the money you give me." And that's how it went after the confession. He had great success, and he deserved it.

The Nontraveling Poor and the Others

Town councils don't look after the traveling poor; it's the fairies who look after them. A clown in a traveling circus who'd had his legs cut off and followed the troupe as a kitchen helper, got an iron chair from a fairy just like one of those in the first-class rows, and which had this special property that whoever sat in it would find a gold louis in his pocket, the way the Wandering Jew found a few coins in his. The circus troupe argued over the chair and thought of nothing else. The gold louis were wasted on orgies and the circus went downhill. One day the chair got smashed by drunks and the unlucky troupe was left to the mercy of the open road. The fairy should have intervened since town councils don't take care of the traveling poor, but the fairy was elsewhere. The acrobats came up with the idea to become nontraveling poor to touch a town council's heart.

The Shadow of Statues

I remember the Grand Bazaar, where I used to be employed. I remember knocking over some trouser buttons into some spectacles and fetching a broom to sweep them up. I also remember a Chinese colleague, who was pink-cheeked and clean-shaven. I wanted to be innovative: display glass inkpots on glass panes. And there was also this: we had a deal with the House of Fichet for cute little safes and safes for dolls. We found out that one of Fichet's sons had died, and, since I was taken for a clever chap, I was asked, if not to go to the funeral to pay the highest respects to the House of Fichet, at least to make a speech which a cute-safe department manager might make. It took me a day to gather the documentation on the firm, a night to prepare the speech, and it was only then that I learned that Monsieur Fichet, who had died and to whom I attributed the most noble social sentiments and other qualities, had hardly had time to have them valued, not being more than three weeks old.

So, then a car stopped outside the hotel in Chartres. To find out who was in that car outside the hotel, whether it was Toto, or whether it was Totel, that's what you'd like to know, but you will never know ... never ... The Parisians' visits have been wonderful for the Chartres hotel owners, but the visits to the Chartres hotels have been very bad for the Parisians, for a number of reasons. A bellhop took the car owner's boots and polished them, but they were polished badly because the huge number of cars coming to the hotels meant that the staff couldn't make the necessary arrangements for proper boot-polishing; it was extremely fortunate that this same huge number of cars prevented our hero from noticing that his boots were polished badly. What had our hero come to do in that ancient city of Chartres, a city so famous? He had come to search for a doctor, because there aren't enough of them in Paris to treat him for all the diseases he had.

More of Those Nontraveling Poor

The town hall steps were packed with poor folk. A lady shook her alms purse right in front of the frock coats coming out: "Give, gentlemen, it's for the poor," and hands dropped in coins of every metallic shade. Then, on the square, the charitable lady's son passed by with the font of all his happiness—a woman his mother hadn't given him; and his mother let out a cry and dashed forward to snatch his happiness away. What happened? I don't know: the charitable lady tripped over onto her hands and the alms purse spilled open. What a scene! The poor folk tumbled over themselves to grab the coins. "Stop thief!" the charitable lady cried out. "Officer, they can't even wait for their money!"

The Swan (Essay in a Witty Style)

The swan is hunted in Germany, the birthplace of Lohengrin. It is used as a logo for a detachable collar in public urinals. Seen on lakes, it's confused with flowers, and one goes into raptures over its boat-like shape; moreover, it is butchered without mercy to make it sing. Painting would be all too willing to make use of the swan, but there isn't any painting around anymore. When it's had time to change into a woman before dying, its flesh is less tough than is the case the other way around: that's when hunters value it most. Under the name of eider, swans have aided eiderdowns. And that's not a bad way to end. Men with long necks, such as Fénelon, the swan of Cambrai, are called cygnet-men or significant men. Etc. . . .

Regrettable News

So, it's true, is it? They're smashing the statues in Place de la Nation. Plaster-of-Paris Eve, who complained behind the chariot, has come moaning with her plaster hair. What are they accusing me of? If I dragged my nephew baby across the carpet, it was to keep him entertained, and there was nothing but laughter behind his tears.

Nocturne of Familial Hesitations ▬▬▬▬▬

There are nights which end in a train station! There are stations which end in the night. Haven't we crossed the tracks at night? The carriage's outside corners were rough with me at night: my deltoid still hurts. While I was waiting for an older sister, or my father, it ended up in something I don't want to admit to: a pair of shoes spattered with bread flour. But I've got a brother who's annoying in stations: he only ever arrives at the last minute (he has his principles), so we have to reopen a suitcase which the servant hasn't even brought yet; even at the ticket counter, he still doesn't know which station he has to direct the coaches to: he's torn between Nogent-sur-Marne and the Ponts-de-Cé, or some other place. The suitcase is here, open! He hasn't bought his ticket and the gas lamps seek in vain to turn night into day or day into night. There are nights which end in a station, stations which end in night. Ah, damned indecision, isn't it you who has led me astray and surely to places very different from waiting rooms? Oh stations!

Fantômas

On the burnished silver door knocker, stained with time, soiled with the dust of time, a sort of Buddha engraved with too high a forehead, droopy ears, and the looks of a seafarer or gorilla: it was Fantômas. He was pulling down on two cords to make something, I don't know what, go up. His foot's slipping; his life depends upon it; he has to reach the apple knocker, the rubber apple before the rat arrives to bite a hole in it. Yet all this is nothing more than engraved silver for a door knocker.

They were as much stuffed shirts as stuffed gourmets, Sir and Madam. The first time the chef came up to them, hat in hand, to ask, "Pardon me, are Sir and Madam satisfied?" They replied, "We'll let you know via the headwaiter." The second time, they didn't answer him. The third time, they contemplated having him thrown out, but they couldn't make up their minds to do so, for as chefs go, he was one of a kind. The fourth time (my God, they lived in the outskirts of Paris, they never saw anyone, they got so bored!), the fourth time they began, "The caper sauce is superb, but the partridge canapé was on the tough side." They went on to talk sport, politics, religion. That was what the chef wanted, for he was none other than Fantômas.

The glass box was painted pink in a manner that made it look like mahogany. The jewelry inside had been stolen, then returned, but by whom? "What do you think?" my mother asked. I looked at the jewels: several clasps, some decorated with stone, others with small watercolors. "I think the thief's insulting us! He's giving us back our jewels because they aren't worth anything. I would have done exactly the same." "That thief is an honest man,'" said my mother, "but as for you . . .'"

A Work of Biography ══════════

Already, at the age of three, the author of these lines was remarkable: he'd make a portrait of the concierge as an Aunt Sally, earthenware color, mouth wide open, at the moment when, eyes full of tears, she was plucking a chicken. The chicken stuck out a platonic neck. But this game of Aunt Sally was just a way to pass the time. All in all, it's remarkable that no one has remarked on him; remarkable, but not regrettable, for if he had been remarked upon, he wouldn't have been remarkable: his career would never have gotten off the ground, which would have been regrettable. It's remarkable that he might have become something to regret, and regrettable that he might have become something to remark upon. Aunt Sally's chicken was a goose.

Game with the Word "Caste"

I'm reconciled with my mother although we're not of the same caste. In Paris, where nothing matters, caste matters. I came across old Vernin, who once owned a bistro which my friends and I wrecked without a second thought because he doesn't belong to our caste, and I drank a glass of wine with him, even if he isn't of my caste. I remember strolling through a certain town with a courtesan who isn't of my caste and who was scorned because of her caste. Nevertheless, since she brought the town to life, there were some who would smile at her, even though she wasn't of their caste. When I was reconciled with my mother, I rubbed and scrubbed her parquet to humiliate myself like someone from another caste, but I ended up scrubbing it black because I don't belong to the caste of scrubbers. The black came from drops of pitch I'd been rubbing in, which made the buffet shed tears. I drank a glass of wine at the family table, but stayed standing, because I'd been scrubbing the parquet.

The Glories of History Require a Reappraisal ▬▬▬

In his youth, Hippolyte Taine didn't disdain, not by a long chalk, to go with the right people, especially of the opposite sex, to see a performance of *La Dame de Chez Maxim's*, but he mostly went with families. He had an overcoat that fit him just right. This overcoat had vertical stripes and a large red stripe, and only one. He often dined with the same family, and they would spend ages deciding what to go and see at the theater. "I've already seen that one," said my sister. "I'll pay Sophie a visit. M. Taine will accompany you." "Will we have time for dinner? It's already half past seven." "Don't worry about that," Taine would reply. "I'm treating all of you to dinner." And it's time he did, we were thinking. But poor Hippolyte had hardly five francs in his pocket, and there were four of us. In the hallway, where we hung our coats, I went up to him: I'd been reading one of his articles which had some Latin words in it and which in a petty, fussy way explained in four stages what makes a good speech. I wanted to express some of my ideas, too, such as the following: "We often don't do justice to someone who has given a lot to his generation because we've never read him, but, conversely, we often give too much recognition to the memory of a man because we haven't read him, with the result that . . ." I would never have believed his face could be so tiny and pale. This little face killed off any desire I had to speak to him.

When one set of gentlemen meets another set, it's rare for their greetings not to be accompanied by smiles. When a set of gentlemen meets a gentleman on his own, if there's one truly courteous greeting, the greetings start to fade away, and sometimes the last in the group doesn't give any greeting at all. It seems I wrote that you bit a woman on her nipple and that blood was dripping. If you believe I did that, why are you even greeting me? And if I believed you'd done that, would I be greeting you? We met at the home of a large lady with glasses and a knitted cape. You shook my hand, but we found ourselves in the room where the lady has her commode, and you threw cushions from the commode at my head. The cushions were very eighteenth century. They say I threw cushions at you, too, instead of exonerating myself. I don't know whether that's true. When my set meets you again, if I'm the last one, the one who doesn't greet you, don't think it's because of the affair with the cushions; but if my set meets yours, and a few smiles are exchanged, don't imagine that any of those smiles is mine.

The Tide Waits for No One

When one of your friends arranges to meet you, if you want to stop him getting one over on you, whether he plans to or not, just don't be there. Leave the meeting place before the appointed time. It's you who will have the advantage, and your honor will remain intact. Which reminds me! At the cubist school, there was a blackboard, a few small black tables, some chalk, and also some tinted Ingres paper, which M. K had plans to make off with. A pupil was waiting but the teacher didn't come, so he left before the time of their meeting. Then the teacher came and left before the time of the meeting. Premeditated one-upmanship or not? *Basta!* The honor of both remained intact.

Paw or Pore Lotion

Against the wall, by the hearth, the man in the red velvet top hat, with a white scar on his cheek, gave me to believe that Sarah Bernhardt had been seen shaving her face. A likely story! Some sailor or other from Belle Isle must have caught her by surprise when she thought she was on her own, wiping away her wrinkles with her paw or pore lotion.

▬▬▬▬▬▬▬▬▬▬▬▬▬

I won't be much longer. I have to answer to the examining magistrate for my friend. Where are the keys? They're not on the sideboard. Excuse me, Your Honor, I have to look for the keys. Ah, here they are! And what a dilemma for the magistrate! He came close to resigning from the case because he was in love with the accused's sister-in-law, but she came to beg him to declare no grounds for prosecution, then she would be his. Deep down, the magistrate is fed up with the whole business. He lingers over certain details: why all these drawings? I launch into a proper course in aesthetics. An artist keeps many works around him so that he can search for forms. Evening falls; the magistrate doesn't know what I'm talking about. He speaks of forgeries. Some friends arrive. The wife of the accused suggests a nice trip by car and the magistrate accepts, hoping the accused will find a way to escape.

To the Memory of Dostoevsky

When the tram had gone over the Saint-Cloud bridge, some-
one, pointing out a shop whose windows were decorated with
paintings on the glass, said, "That's where all those things go
on!" I found out what went on there. There was a former actor,
a little old, retired actor all shriveled up and threadbare, who,
by reading paperback novels, had ended up confusing them
with reality. He had seen that a person could procure children
of a very young age to sell on to old men. He believed this and
did it. When I got to his place, a small blonde was on the bench
as if she were at school. She was trustfully admiring a dreadful
cheap doll. There was a certain old woman, fat Melanie—one
would never have believed that a former actor could have a
grandmother younger than himself—a certain old woman who,
in spite of the child's tears, insisted on undressing the doll. So
far it was nothing more than a doll being undressed, that is to
say the chief attraction of the show. The former actor procured
children for himself or did the buying for others, though he
made use of them himself, too. All this is horrible, and what is
worse is that I found fat Melanie at one of my closest friend's.
She was sorting out the accounts with him. They didn't want
to let me in because the gentleman was working, but I saw fat
Melanie.

True Anecdote

The triumph of Mlle Ratkine's performance at the Franklin Theatre in St. Petersburg was interrupted by screams. The unfortunate singer had fallen into the orchestra pit and broken her arm. In my capacity as a doctor, I was the one who went to look for the beautiful lady, found she'd fainted, and had her carried to her dressing room. The director was in love with her, that much was obvious: he kept walking up and down outside the room without daring to go in or even knock. At last, he's knocking! No answer: "No doubt her little French lover is with her," he tells me. Her lover! Alas, the injured lady was at the mercy of the old stage manager, who took advantage of the fact that one of Mlle Ratkine's hands was free to kiss it feverishly, with no risk of getting a slap.

Valiant Warrior on Foreign Soil ▬▬▬

Olga de Berchold has left for the camp to join the one she loves: Verchoud the soldier. The soldier goes off to war. Olga follows him and suffers on the journey. Verchoud is taken prisoner. Olga goes to cash in her fortune and returns to pay the ransom: she's too suspicious to pay it all at once. The ransom paid, Verchoud falls ill. Olga nurses him and for the first time declares her love. The soldier tells her she's not the one he loves, but a certain peasant woman he's only caught a glimpse of and never spoken to. He dies. Olga is ruined, desperate: what will become of her? She goes in search of the peasant woman.

At the Chauffeurs' Get-Together

Our wives were seated on the other bench. I recognized my place, near the books and papers. I recognized the glow of dawn on the houses opposite, but I couldn't tell if it was very early or very late. We were talking about a book called *The Little Geese* by Herrmayer and about its author, Cabalis or Andral. Herrmayer is his alias: it's a marvelous book. We stole canned desserts from the restaurant owner. There were dried figs on the plates of those who don't like figs. We swopped figs and grapes, but as we were carrying off the canned desserts, a voice said: "Oh, no! Hey, not that! That's my cook's outfit and bedsheets!"

The Key

When the lord of Framboisy came back from the war, his wife sternly rebuked him in church, and so he said: "Madame, here is the key to all I own. I'm leaving for good." Out of discretion, the lady let the key drop to the church floor. A nun in a corner was praying because she'd lost her own key, the one to the convent, and nobody could get in. "So, let's see if your lock will let this one fit inside." But the key was no longer there. It was already in the Cluny Museum. It was a huge key in the shape of a tree trunk.

True Miracles

That good old priest! After he left us, we witnessed him flying over the lake like a bat. He was so engrossed in his own thoughts, he didn't even notice the miracle. The bottom of his cassock was wet. It was this which astonished him.

The Soldier from Marathon

There's a fair at the asylum for psychiatrists. By evening, the paths in the grounds are taken over by well-intentioned but slightly apprehensive crowds. Here and there are little wooden tables with a candle protected in a glass, where sweets are sold: everything went along just as it should until, during the theater show put on by the inmates, one of them who was playing the role of some sir or lord or suchlike, began flinging himself to the ground in a celebrated pose, crying, "It's me, the soldier from Marathon!" A few people there had to cut him short and restore him to reason, to the present, to those present, to precedence, but no one dared wield a stick because of the present, those present, and precedence.

The Aunt, the Tart, and the Hat ▬▬▬▬

When I used to work in a store, I shared a small three-roomed apartment with a colleague. We were so tired we never quarreled, but we spent a lot of time discussing whose clothes were whose: a pair of trousers was found in the living room and we had to come to a decision about them. One day in the store something happened: my friend came in with part of his beard chopped off. That same day he had to deliver a package to a part of town where I also had some business. Not without thinking the matter over for quite some time, I took charge of this package. We talked a lot about the best metro line to take, and the question of the fare grew quite heated. That evening in the store, my friend invited us to dinner at his aunt's. This aunt was a former actress, not quite very old, who squeezed herself into a corset, and who, once a year, made herself a small hat in the shape of a tart, which she rushed to put on whenever we begged her to sing. She sang the repertoire of Theresa. For a bit of fun, we were served a tart in the shape of a small hat. There was a smooching couple at the table. "I know all about that," said the old lady, "but you, my beautiful girl, do you know what you're getting yourself into?" The beautiful girl was all of forty. She replied that she had a grown son, a grown daughter, and that she loved young people.

A Point of Law

Yes, but they'd forgotten about the carriage! It was the day of the bankruptcy, and the coachman came up the stairs: they owed the coachman sixty francs, sixty-six centimes. He'd been waiting sixty hours. He climbed the wooden stairs with a heavy tread. Now a bunch of friends were sitting around the table, having a laugh, but the official receiver had set a percentage for the coachman, since the coachman was grouped with the other creditors at the fixed rate, i.e., 4½ percent of the total owed. Soon there were intimidating figures on the wooden staircase: the coachman had asked for witnesses to be sent to the receiver, the police commissioner having declared himself incompetent when it came to commercial law.

Unsentimental Education[5]

A ladder doesn't hold as fast as a Virginia creeper does. My old Greek teacher lives here. I've come to say farewell. We're in the living room, with its carpet half-rotted away, and his lady wife, who is very practical-minded, says to me: "In this life you'll need to earn five francs a minute . . . no, that'd be too much, but at least every three minutes." "My wife is certainly practical-minded," says the Greek teacher.

American Christomathy at 3.50 ===

The black in the window alternated with white. It's Sunday, officially and by name, but not in the foreign lady's heart. The white horse crosses the room in a flowery gallop: there are more spearheads than flags. The foreign lady, sequestered behind the scene, flicks through the canvases. Foreign ladies seem sad when they can't speak French: they have a sharp eye, but they wear their dress-collars too high. This is the invention, she says, of "detachable faith," an article on sale all over the world, easy to carry around with you, most of all for Satan and his crew. The foreign lady won't make use of this detachable faith until she speaks French fluently: she's happy for the moment to be its inventor.

Aristo Art

Femina magazine describes the Duchess of H's stately home as an awfully sad-looking building, and its author lingers over a depiction of the courtyard's reddish-gray paving. He tells us that the middle room is occupied by an old servant who watches over the home in summer. What's astonishing is that the curtains still drag a little on the floor like a dress with a train, and he confesses that, being a novelist, he's always carefully observed other stately homes in the region, where the curtains also drag on the floor. He has witnessed an altercation, or half altercation, between a daughter and her mother on the subject of physics or physique, the maid having asked if they made much of physics or physique at the boarding school where her own son was sent. A slap was dealt like a certain round leaf, very similar to watercress leaves that grow on walls. I've mentioned the servant who watches over the house in summer. It's the servant who takes care of the garbage. The duchess has an aristocratic profile, and the wall plant is called aristolochia. The author of the article is called Aristide.

The Concarneau Regatta

The drowned don't always sink to the bottom. It's enough if you're in trouble in the water to remember that you once knew how to swim, and you'll see your trousers jerk around like a puppet's legs. At the Concarneau regatta, that's what happened to me. I stayed perfectly calm before sinking, or else those smart skiffs going by would have noticed my struggles or even ... in short, a certain optimism. The shore so near! With life-sized Israelite figures there, and of the most gracious demeanor. What surprised me coming out of the water was to find I was hardly wet at all, and to be looked upon not as everyone's lap-dog, but as a human being.

Sir Elizabeth (Pronounced *Sœur*) ▬▬▬

The town of Happney is in ruins, alas! All that remains is a wall
between two square towers, two towers that look like farm-
houses or water tanks. They were once places of learning: now
they're empty! All that remains ... All that remains is a stable
door and some cracks, alas, and the cobblestones overgrown
with brambles. The stationmaster is still there, however, the
one who told me the story of Sir Elizabeth. Sir Elizabeth was
of the female sex, but she had to turn herself into a working
man. Sir Elizabeth entered a poetry competition. At that time,
in America, the female sex couldn't conceive of themselves as
poets. Sir Elizabeth was crowned poet laureate and became
eligible for a double-bust on each side of the stable door. The
door's still there; the two busts have been eroded by the weather,
alas! Sir Elizabeth was stirred by the sculptor who had made
her bust, and revealed her sex to him, but the sculptor repulsed
her because she had deceived the town. And so it was that Sir
Elizabeth joined the army and got herself killed.

I will never get away: I rush to say goodbye to my aunt and there's my family under the lamplight; they hold me back with a thousand pieces of advice. My suitcase is packed, but my suit is still at the cleaner's. When I arrive at the cleaner's, I can hardly recognize it: it isn't mine. Someone has changed it! No, that is my suit, but horribly baggy, mutilated, stretched, stitched up again, hemmed in black. Outside on the street, two delicious Breton women are laughing near a laundry cart: I really don't have time to follow them. Damn! But they're going the same way as me in the night. I see that the names of the streets have changed; now in Lorient there's one called "Lyrical Energy" street. What amazing town council could give such a name to the streets at night? At the hotel it occurs to me that I should check the bill from the cleaner's: 325 francs. They will send the suit onto me. Am I going mad? The café's full of curious people. I meet a painter from Paris, difficult to shake off. He adores me here, even though we get on each other's nerves elsewhere: I'm so late I forgo embracing him, and now no cab! While they're trying to find one for me, some childhood friends beg me to stop off at Le Mans! No, not Le Mans, at Nogent! No not at Nogent because we're very much on the wrong side of . . . ah, my God! I'm losing the thread of everything . . . I end up cadging a ride with a transporter of pianos. And the cleaner? Here I am in a strange suit, all told quite distinguished: this gray frockcoat bursting open because of the excess of underwear I have on me to make my suitcase lighter! This top hat, what a way to travel. Ah! I've forgotten to say goodbye to . . . And the cleaner? I've let the time for the train's departure slip by, the only train: everything will have to start all over again tomorrow! I shan't sleep the whole night!

Parisian Literature

The memoirs of Madame Sarah Bernhardt or any of her women comrades. They begin with a description of the countryside where you'll find words in dialect. The moor is called the *chigne*, as in the Franche-Comté region, and the wood thicket is called the *chignon*.

Robert gets lost in the park. He meets the lords of the manor. He would accept their friendly invitation, but he is expected elsewhere. Elsewhere, in reality, they are not waiting for him. He is surprised to find his father among the inhabitants of Chartres.

Robert's name was more likely Hippolyte. He would have been dressed in the latest fashion, if there had been a latest fashion, but there isn't a latest fashion, so he was dressed like everyone else, that is to say, badly. Robert would have been capable of doing eight hundred kilometers by car to go and say to the friend of one of his friends: "Mr. So-and-So sends his greetings to you," for Robert was good, but he didn't have any friends.

Robert sat down at the table and ate as he hadn't eaten for a long time; that is to say, he ate little, for he always ate a lot. Have I said that he ate well? Well, he ate averagely most of the time, but it was all the same to him. Robert didn't do anything in order not to waste time working. He wasted time perhaps in other ways. If he had some task to undertake, he wouldn't have known how to see it through, and he wouldn't have lifted a finger to do so. Robert did nothing, which is better than doing wrong, and this did not prevent him from doing things wrongly. But let's leave Robert in Chartres.

Literary Manners

A merchant from Havana sent me a cigar wrapped in gold, which someone had already smoked a bit. The poets around the table said it was to ridicule me, but the old Chinese man who'd invited us said that this was the custom in Havana when they wanted to truly honor a person. I showed everyone two magnificent poems a learned friend of mine had translated and written down for me because I'd admired his oral translation. The poets said that these poems were well known and worthless. The old Chinese man said they couldn't know the poems since there was only one manuscript of them in existence, and that was in Pahlavi, a language they didn't know. So, the poets burst into loud laughter like children and the old Chinese man watched us with a sad expression.

The Merciless Laugh of the Boa Constrictor

The railway station of Creil is a hub, they say, for products manufactured in the north. The Oise flows past some barrels; the riverbank path is very similar to your sidewalks, boulevard Pasteur. I'm amazed to see that the barrels conceal a fat old idiot of a woman taking care of her fetus. Her, the violated woman! Her, the mother! The iron bridge is a cage—the train passes so fast over the iron bridge—and down below, the Oise with its fishermen and their rods! What idiotic scenery! Two graves? No, I saw her again, the hideous old weeping woman. I saw her at a fair in front of the junk stalls; the crowd of women in their long skirts were buying garish toys. The violator is serenading her with his violin: the violated woman is flying high.

So, it's true then! Here I am like Philoctetes! Abandoned by a ship on an unknown rock because my foot hurts. The unlucky part is that my trousers were torn off by the sea. Having made inquiries, it turns out I'm on the shores of England. "I'll find a policeman straightaway!" And that's what happened: a police-man appeared speaking in French: "You don't recognize me," he said in that language, "I'm your English maid's husband!" There was a reason I didn't recognize him—I've never had an English maid. He led me to a nearby town, covering my naked-ness as best he could with leaves, and from there to a tailor's. And when I offered to pay: "No point," he said, "secret police funds" or "secret polite fun"—I couldn't quite figure out what he said.

The Spirit of the *Mona Lisa*

The *Mona Lisa*! It's the baroness's alarm clock! It has the spirit of the *Mona Lisa*. It stops and starts to keep up with the adventures of that unhappy picture. The police could have consulted it some time ago. It would have responded like certain tables do to believers in the spirits. This clock comes from Florence or the Black Forest. It lives in a mahogany or copper colonnade and never leaves the side of the traveling baroness. The clock rings, the beauty wakes and considers. It's said that the spirit of the *Mona Lisa* inspires the baroness's beautiful poems and paintings, and that its great spring will be broken forever when she decides to take a new lover. The *Mona Lisa* doesn't need to be rewound to return to the routine of its ticking. In any case, the chambermaid secretly helps with the fairy spells. Nobody helps the baroness with her fairy spells, except the *Mona Lisa* herself, whose mysterious smile keeps watch by her bedside through the night.

The Situation of Maids in Mexico ▬▬▬▬▬▬

for Guillaume Apollinaire

The investigation into the situation of maids in Mexico, under-taken by the *Mercure de France* for the satisfaction of its learned readers, troubles every thinking person. The illustrated supple-ment to the *Petit Parisien* shows the much-gossiped-about Marie T in her slip in her attic room at the moment when, with her two white arms, she makes a supreme effort to hide from her employer a pile of kitchen utensils barely concealed by a dirty sheet. The *Journal des Gens de Maison* responds to the *Mercure de France*'s report with a counter investigation into the masters and mistresses, and we find out a few juicy titbits about them! A certain Amélie B had managed to hide one of her cousins, who was anemic and unemployed, in a Renaissance chest at the house of M. and Mme M. The cousin was regularly visited by a doctor, and was even quite demanding, and com-plained of too much noise in the house, and of certain poker games that prevented him from sleeping. Mme M, who keeps an illicit portion of her earnings in the chest, has no choice but to put up with the presence of the stranger. As for M. M, he is not unaware of the presence of the anemic, unemployed cousin in the Renaissance chest, but if his dignity prevents him from offering Amélie's cousin a more comfortable place to stay, the love which they say he has for her prevents him from having the man kicked out.

The editor of the *Journal des Gens de Maison* audaciously aspires through his own writings to match the *Mercure de France*. He adds appropriately, if not with great originality, that "we do not depend on that which we do not seem to depend on, nor on that we want to depend on, nor on that we seek not to depend on and which we seem to depend on, but we depend upon ourselves." He adds, "We depend more on that which we do not seem in any way to depend on." In this manner, the question of the maids in Mexico is resolved.

Fable without a Moral

There was once a locomotive so polite it would stop to let walkers across. One day an automobile came jolting onto the railway line. The driver whispered into the ear of his mount, "Aren't we going to lodge a complaint?" "It's young," said the locomotive, "and doesn't know any better." The locomotive went no further than spitting a tiny puff of scornful steam onto the breathless sportsman.

Since, in spite of the arms they throw around shoulders, the gold *louis* and the banknotes they toss at young women are protected by reinforced revolvers in their waistcoats, Jérôme Paturot renounced café life despite his intimate relationship with Mac Farlane himself. He founded a bank, a limited company for the buying and distribution of the works of Greco to shareholders, but this only showed how the value of paintings can fluctuate. There are days when a Raphaël is worth no more than thirty sous. So, he became a catalog editor for fashion houses; now here he should have made himself familiar with the relevant literature to set up a store for our fashionable women. He would have been a fruit-and-veg seller for all seasons, except we don't have seasons anymore!

The Explosion of the Grand Cross

The burial had already taken place the day before, but they had to start all over again owing to a mistake in the funeral route. Rue Royale, another incident; one of the hearse's wheels comes off. The master of ceremonies makes the best of it. He takes the wreaths with the same hand that's holding his cane. One read, "*To my master, Catulle Mendès.*" Another read, "*To our young friend too discreet to share his troubles with us.*"

And the young girl who looked after him so well! She was weeping, weeping, her blond hair in veils.

But that evening, he really had to go to play his part in the Porte-Saint-Martin theater show. He preferred his southern-style hairstyle and beard to an Egyptian mask cut away at the chin, but the beard caught fire and the grand cross went up in flames.

The Press

I went inside hesitantly: there was an ostrich that was losing its feathers, and on a white stucco plaster was a bronze bird whose plumage was depicted by a series of engraved shells. It was M. Abel Hermant, or someone of the same sort as M. Abel Hermant, who appeared as soon as the hall was opened. "Ah young man!" he said, "you've come for a bit of cash!" Later I learned that everyone who went there was given a bit of cash. At the word cash, the ostrich shed one of its feathers and the bronze bird flew off. Anyway, the hall was dusty and deserted. They kept pins there in iron boxes painted with the portraits of great men: Cuvier, Buffon, etc. "Ah, young man," repeated M. Abel Hermant, or someone of that sort, "you've come for a bit of cash!" And the birds began their motions again. "No, monsieur! It's free! It's a free outlet." My future spiritual mentor wouldn't hear any more of it. "Free outlet" enlightened him, and he turned his back on me. The ostrich put on its gendarme's cap and watched me with curious anxiety. The bronze bird was bronzer than bronze.

With the cleansing of the streambed, the fish of the brook Cedron have died, despite the protection of the Almighty. The courtesan standing beside the deconsecrated stream made this bed her own, but she ate of the fish, and despite the protection of the Almighty, and as this fish was cleansed, she died.

Cinematograph

A family from the provinces in a carriage: it's pretty amazing that the two maids are on top. Then they're on the seat, then on the running boards, where they fall asleep. Meanwhile, two thieves climb on top and get up to some odd tricks. They attach cardboard ears to everyone asleep, and the next morning, monsieur, madame, and the maids will no longer recognize one another.

Mutual Disdain for the Castes ━━━━━━━

Where else but the animal tamer's! In a hall full of cardboard shoeboxes, the man himself appeared, or rather it was his own portrait by Van Dongen: in a black-and-white costume whose leather embellishments were golden brown. His poorly painted eyes were huge, and his hair hung down like the wings of a *chocarneau* (that's a bird with curly feathers). The animal tamer offered me some tobacco, and commended me to his wife, a faded blonde. "You've never been inside a cage?" "Yes, as the animal," she told me. I didn't understand. She explained that they rented a large furnished apartment in each town so that they could spend the five hundred francs they earned daily. "We keep nothing for ourselves! Nothing! Look! Those shoes! A few books and that's all! So, we won't be inviting you to stay for dinner." The tamer of big beasts returned and seemed surprised to see me still there. I believe he was also an animal dentist.

Another Point of Law

On the Quai des Flammes, the lame man drew my attention to the counter-letter in tiny Chinese writing. My correspondent informed me he was sending me five thousand francs, adding that he would go to one of my suppliers to be repaid in a certain number of meters of cream- or crime-colored faille silk. Why was the writing so small and in Chinese, if not to get around the rule of law, or my law. The law of the most powerful! I continued my walk along the quay. My mother was lighting a fire with cork. My aunt looked well and wasn't saying a word. "My aunt has a healthy complexion!" "No!" my mother said. "That's her natural color." I didn't say anything about the counter-letter in Chinese. Does the counter-letter in Chinese have the natural complexion of commerce, or is it a healthy complexion? It has the natural complexion of obligatory illness.

During the time of the Great Irish Famine, a man in love declared passionately to a widow: "A quick veal scallop, my heavenly one!" "No" said the widow, "I don't want to spoil this figure which you honor with your admiration!" But she sent for her child and cut a nice bloody piece out of him where the veal would be. Would the child bear the scar for life? I don't know. He screamed biblically when they cut the veal out of him.

The Beggar Woman of Naples

When I lived in Naples, there was a beggar woman at the entrance to my palace, to whom I'd toss a coin or two before getting into my carriage. One day, surprised she'd never thanked me, I looked at her more closely. It was then I saw that what I'd taken for a beggar woman was a wooden crate painted green, containing some red soil and a few half-rotten bananas . . .

In the Hill Country ══════════════

I came to a hill covered by a meadow on top; it was surrounded by trees, and you could see other hills nearby. I found my father at the hotel, who told me: "I've brought you here to marry you off." "But I haven't got my black suit!" "That doesn't matter; you're getting married, that's the main thing." I walked toward the church and saw that my intended was a pale young lady. In the afternoon, I was struck by the charm of the celebrations; there were benches placed around the meadow; couples were arriving, some nobles, a few learned folk, some school friends, where the ground dipped under the trees. It made me want to draw it. And my wife? Ah, so it was only a joke, after all. You don't get married in the English fashion without a black suit. The mayor was head of the local school. He made a speech, facing the meadow, announcing that the wedding was off, because everyone knew the state of our finances. And so I choked back sobs of humiliation, and wrote this page, along with much other literature worthy of ridicule.

Capital: Table Mat

The little girl has breasts too far apart. They'll need to be taken care of in Paris. Any delay would be in bad taste. But in Paris all the shops look the same: crystal and gold: hat doctor! watch doctor! Where's the breast doctor?

In 1889, the trenches were set in wax under glass: two thousand meters underground, two thousand Poles in chains didn't know what they were doing there: the French nearby discovered an Egyptian shield: they showed it to the greatest doctor in the world, the one who invented ovariotomy. The greatest tenor in the world sang two thousand notes in the theater which has a two-thousand-meter tower: he earned two million and gave it to the Pasteur Institute. The French were under glass.

What Comes Out of the Flute

The wounded traveler died on the farm and was buried under the trees on the driveway. One day a rat popped out of his grave; a passing horse reared up. So the rat ran away, leaving behind a half-eaten photo. The traveler's last request was to be buried with this image of a lady in a lowcut dress. The rider who saw it fell in love with the model on the strength of his faith in her image.

Dénouement

The smoke from the steamboat darkened the whole sky and blocked out the sun.

Just like Saint Anne, a woman by the bottom of the chimney was dying upright in a nun's habit. Her skin was like paper, and all the lines on her face were those of irony and mourning. Oh, Saint Anne, try to smile, for here is your son: His Lordship the Duke of Orléans. It's he himself, recaptured by the Mexican pirate who's here in the full costume of the Steppes.

Oh, smoke! Smoke! Steamboat! Darken the light from the sun!

His Lordship the Duke of Orléans has a wonky eye, his white eye, a false collar, fashionable in 1895, a large frockcoat, and close-cropped hair. His Lordship the Duke of Orléans offers Saint Anne a sheet of paper covered in penciled lines.

"I am obliged to you for my son, etc. . . . ," which leaves the pirate confused, the pirate with sequins round his stage hat.

SECOND PART

Moral Death

The old man, who carried a lit lamp underneath his great black cloak lined with fur, raised eyes full of tears toward the stained-glass window. The organ bore away the dead. The stained-glass window repeated the story of the seven vertical skies, and it was the harmony of all florae. Our Lord crowned with pearls and without His miter changed the course of time to end His warnings.

Solitary Equatorials

The four knotty toes serve as curls for the lofty bull who is no more than a man fighting—down! The stoves are homes which don't pay their taxes on doors or windows—arise! Tongues or trunks emerge from them. On the steps that step for they are all the roaming creatures of creation, the Buddha, who lends dignity to a sheet of paper bordered with gold, hangs onto a purse with the idea of making necklaces for later. Don't be alarmed! It's no more than a border—get a grip! But with a double entendre. It's rained so much on all this a thorn has grown there, piercing through with brazen or bizarre solicitude. A million miles . . . a million smiles.

A Student's Life

The streetcar in this faraway suburb stopped all too often. I realized the driver was reporting to the shopkeepers about some commissions they'd assigned him for the city. A small girl in a bakery was weighed down by a ledger. Finally, my friend and I arrived at the Turk's: a big blue building with signs hanging down on all sides: department eiderdowns, down pillows, etc. . . . The Turk had a severe and indulgent pince-nez, a short beard parted like that of Henry IV, but with a clay pipe and bare legs whose eczema revealed his nationality. One of my school pals had got there first. It was here I learned that Max Jacob's mathematical compositions were so awful that everyone had given up correcting them, and moreover that the Turk was absolutely remarkable, a true refined character from a novel. The Turk showed us some drag clothes for sale—a tailcoat cut from an old cashmere shawl—and told me about his family who would be so happy to know I was nicely dressed. Twenty francs! My friend and I wandered about for a long time outside the house, and we decided not to knock again before dark. The Turk opened up for us half an hour later. He was busy with a gentleman and a lady who seemed to us the epitome of chic. Today I suspect that Turk of conducting a dishonorable trade.

Short Poem

I remember my playroom. The muslin curtains on the window patterned with white trimmings. I tried to find the alphabet in them, and when I could make out the letters, I would transform them into imagined drawings. H, a man sitting; B, the arch of a bridge over a river. In the room were several chests with open flowers lightly sculpted into their wood. But what I liked best were two balls on columns I could see behind the curtains, which I thought of as the heads of puppets I wasn't allowed to play with.

The Name

In the old garden was a whitebeard: in the grotto, the secretary was writing. They asked him:

"Is it true that Diane has a child and that the man who has lived with her for fifteen years knows nothing of it?"

"Sir, Diane is my wife, and our child is with my mother!"

The secretary went on to name Diane's pals—a bunch of hooligans! And you could see she partly led a double life. Monsieur Jean unfortunately repeated the secretary's revelations, and a new existence began for Monsieur Jean. Diane was not unaware that he knew about her life, and she looked at him with eyes full of fury. One day she spilt some water over him, believing it to be boiling when it was only hot. Having failed with her experiment, she went around the garden with hotter water. Her friends surrounded her, seeming afraid of some catastrophe. Finally, two city agents led her away in a cab. She was obliged to tell them her name.

"Diane the Old Bag!"

"That's not a name!"

"If you come with me, you'll be inside Diane the Old Bag's house. And, Monsieur Brigadier, just for you I'll whisper my name in your ear . . . Adele Schmidt! I'm Italian!"

Ah, how her looks changed for Monsieur Jean when he learned her true name. She really did have the face of an Italian with the name of Schmidt. He told his friends the name and it floated around her in whispers.

The Centaur

Yes! I've met the centaur! It was on a road in Brittany: round trees were scattered on the slopes. He's the color of milky coffee: he has lustful eyes and his rump is more a snake's tail than a horse's body. I felt too weak to speak to him, and my family was watching us from a distance, more frightened than me. Sun, what mysteries you light up around you!

In the Silent Forest

In the silent forest, night has not yet fallen, and the storm of misery has not yet offended the leaves. In the silent forest which the dryads have fled, to which the dryads will return no more.

In the silent forest, the stream no longer ripples, for it flows almost without water and turns.

In the silent forest, there is a tree black as black, and behind the tree there's a bush with the shape of a head, and it's on fire, a fire in flames of blood and gold.

In the silent forest, where the dryads will return no more, there are three black horses, the three horses of the wise men, and the wise men are no longer on their horses, nor elsewhere, and the horses speak with the voices of men.

A Great Man Needs No Manservant

In a meadow, under the trees, sits the king in a sheet skirt while a feast of lobsters is prepared. His housekeeper, Mme Casimir, the natural daughter of a noble, and noble in her ways, greets him in her usual manner with her hump and her eighty years: "Well then, is everything all right, Madame Casimir?" "Oh, you know me, Sire," said the old Parisian. "As long as I've got a few coins on me, I feel quite young again." Meanwhile the feast of lobsters led to people coming in through the roof, to conversations with legs dangling from skylights, and to frying pans catching fire.

Kaleidoscope ▬▬▬▬▬▬▬▬▬▬▬▬▬▬▬▬

It all looked like a mosaic: the animals walked with their paws to the sky except for the donkey whose white belly bore written words which kept changing. The tower was an opera glass; there were gold-embroidered tapestries depicting black cows; and the little princess in a black dress—we couldn't tell if her dress had green suns, or if we were looking at it through ragged holes.

Errors of Mercy

I'd rather go to prison with him than let him escape. And so be it! We're in a big tower. One night in my sleep, reaching out to take hold of him, I touched nothing more than a white foot rising to the ceiling, and here I am alone in the tower. From the tops of their big haycarts, the farmers stare at me through the window, forgiveness in their eyes.

Surprises

The mileposts on the Murcie roads are lingams. The red-haired vagabond man of letters approached the illustrated magazines to "find out more." They all showed the Moulin Rouge in Paris, women sleeping with men, looking as if they were alive; and they came to him on the path where he was lost, and they came to him from the washerwoman who sold him some burnt potatoes, and they came to him from boulevard Saint-Martin where the bistro steps and the table sweets oversaw twenty revolutions per century and one mid-Lent festival per year.

The Feminist Question

Without admitting it, he was afraid that one day she'd get it wrong with her animals. When she was at the foot of the tower, this frail romantic amazon brought her galloping horse to a halt, went inside, massaged her fiancé, then whistled for her mount, by now far away, to return, and it did. That Mademoiselle de Valombreuse was a masseuse, her fiancé could well forgive, but that she was an animal tamer was too much.

The Painting's Background

It's a small country party, a small party near a well. The poor child is alone on the beach, on the sloping rocks of the dune, and one could say she has a halo over her head. Oh, I know how to save her, big and fat as I am, I run, run toward her. Over there by the well they're playing the Marseillaise, and me, I come running to save her. I haven't yet mentioned the sky's color because I wasn't sure that with the sea it wasn't just all one big smooth painting in that color of school slate boards with chalk marks, yes, with a diagonal chalk streak like the blade of a guillotine.

That

Everything was low! Everything was heavily padded and covered, and it was all warm and stuffy. I was lying on some sofa cushions and daydreaming: he was writing at his low, heavy table. Then between us appeared the goddess, the transparent goddess with her green helmet. And she stayed there until the servant came in, with his smell, alas!

When will the gravediggers return to Ophelia's tomb? Ophelia is still not inside her immortal tomb: it's the gravediggers who'll be put there if the white horse wishes it so. And the white horse? He comes every day to nibble among the stones. It's the white horse from the White Horse Inn in front of the tomb. He has thirty-six ribs. The tomb is an open window on mystery.

Spanish Generosity

The King of Spain used a Spanish friend of mine to gift me with three large diamonds on a shirt, a lace collar on a bullfighter's jacket, a wallet containing guidance on how to live one's life. Carriages, boulevards, dropping in on friends! Will the maid sleep with me? M. S. L. offered his hand to G. A., who refused it for no reason. I've patched things up with the Ys . . . Now that I'm here at the National Library I realize I'm under surveillance. Each time I attempt to read certain books, four employees advance toward me with dolls' swords. In the end, a young pageboy comes up to me. "Come this way!" he says. He shows me a pit hidden behind the books; he shows me a wooden wheel which looks like an instrument of torture. "You're condemned to death for reading books on the Inquisition!" And I see that on my sleeve they've sewn a skull: "How much do you want?" I say. "How much can you give?" "Fifteen francs." "That's too much," says the pageboy. "I'll give them to you on Monday." The King of Spain's generosity had drawn the attention of the Inquisition.

It's the Depth Which Disappoints Least

Can one plant a beech tree in such a small garden? The doors and windows of the seven neighboring workshops touch each other in the little yard where we find ourselves, my brother and me. The beech tree seed is a slightly rotten banana or a potato. There are some old women who are not happy with us. But if the beech tree grows, won't it be too big, and if it doesn't grow, what's the point of planting it? Yet while they were planting it, my friends found the precious stones I'd lost.

Disdain for Some Things and Not Others ▬▬▬

The swan from Andersen's fairy tale was approaching the river harbor. Our quincunxes were full of nobility, and below the green mountainside the old suburbs sheltered the workers. My friend the romantic poet and I were on the quay near the washerwomen, holding out bread to the swan from Andersen's fairy tale. The disdainful swan didn't bother with the bread, and the swan didn't take enough notice of the noise of your clothes-beating, oh washerwomen, nor of the distant noise of your quarrels, you workers hanging about in doorways after your meal.

Two Lives

I knew Dumoulin when I was a science student at the posh high school: he seemed a fool to those who only care for appearances, he had a big heart, and was fixed in his ways. Since I enjoyed lying in bed in the mornings and making up stories about my friends, here's what I imagined for Dumoulin.

Dumoulin hung out with a former ship's captain, an autograph collector who had a sick child. Dumoulin chewed his nails in front of Miklowa Anastasia Verounoff, who was passing through Paris. The Russian woman was well read in literature, which made Dumoulin impatient, and, since she was a bit off with him, he turned the conversation to dance in the hope of getting through to her that way. Mme Michel, the sailor's wife, came in holding the sick child.

"It could be a Millet . . . really!" said Anastasia. Dumoulin left and the other life began.

"None of you earns a thing!" said his mother at home. "I was really happy when you got into the posh high school, but it doesn't bring in any money. We've lost our lawsuit, and your brother is a good-for-nothing. It won't be him who feeds us. The hospital, the hospital—that's what's in store for us."

You just had to listen and resign yourself to growing sad.

Three months later Dumoulin got set up in a factory in Brittany. He was loved by the employees, consulted by the owner, and his mother could take baths. One day he fell asleep on the point of forgetting . . . forgetting.

Is the Sun Pagan?

The woodcutter, near the church porch in the place where the grapevine and grazing stag are carved, the woodcutter sent the cracked wood to a sunray, and the sunray responded by sending him back the cracked wood. The fight grew so heated that the woodcutter, straightening up, said, "I can't stand it anymore!" Putting his jacket back on, he went into the church. The Sun followed him as far as it could with a long stick, but the Sun is a pagan with no right to enter a nave.

The horse has trouble breathing: the drug they gave him to work up some zeal has messed up their plan. And there's still no sign of the idols at the top of the mountains. The stupid idiot kept kicking his horse's flank, and the universe was no bigger than a gourd. A smoking banner marked the native soil. Retreat? No one ever got out of here. Advance? Alas, the horse is even now dying on the spot. But now we can hear strains of music in the air; it's as if they were on fire with ideals. Spring is playing bowls with the trees, and the valley vomits out forty foals.

The Elite's Two Audiences

The day of the great steeplechase, the queen mother wore blue velvet stockings. Near a barrier, the king's mistress went up to him and said: "Prince, this woman is not your mother: she's a usurper with no rights to the throne!" The king made a long speech in praise of prostitution, and married his mistress, a prostitute. A bespectacled servant who slept in the kitchen on a decorated porcelain stove was happy about the marriage. What does the public think of the elite? The first audience found his speech on prostitution long-winded, the other audience applauded loudly.

Wanted to draw water from the pump into two blue pots; grew dizzy because of the ladder's height; returned because I had one pot too many and didn't go back to the pump because of my dizziness; went out to buy a tray for my lamp because it was leaking oil; found no trays except for a square tea tray, unsuitable for lamps, and left without a tray. Headed for the public library and realized on the way that I had two false collars on and no tie; went back home; went to M. Vildrac's to request a magazine and refused it because inside the magazine M. Jules Romains speaks ill of me. Had no sleep because of my remorse, my remorse and despair.

Metempsychosis

Here darkness and silence! Pools of blood in the shape of clouds. Bluebeard's seven wives are no longer in the cupboard. Nothing remains of them except this organdy wimple. But over there! Over there on the ocean are seven galleys, seven galleys whose topsail ropes hang down into the sea like braids onto a woman's shoulders. Here they come! Here they come! They're here!

Picture of the Fair

Day of the fair in Quimper. Chestnut trees shelter the riverbanks at dusk, and from such a height! The riverbanks are full of people. In the square are the stallholders. Since the captain was really drunk, I led him to the café on Chestnut Quay. Here, away from the noise, I comforted him: a little coffee to revive his spirits.

My child, my sister, today you're crying: you miss the Quimper fair. Ah, you were pampered back then, that's for sure. It reminds you of the evening they opened the menagerie just for you. At dusk, my sister, for you alone we went from caravan to caravan in search of the cub sick of being a tiger's son. The stallholders were dining, the cub whining: they said he was consumptive. The father tiger was plain as a swallow. Now that you're married, today you weep, my sister. Those stallholders are in Marseilles now: the sea down there is bluish-gray wood. There's a hinge on the coast, a ship is painted in the background—so dismal, so dismal! A woman has a handkerchief the color of a ripe orange. Her husband wants to take a shot at her. My child, my sister, think back on sweeter times . . .[6]

The Shot

Oh, I daren't find out! I don't want to know! No! I can't make up my mind to get out of bed and find out! The shot! The shot! Yesterday evening he was so sad: his poor money! His poor heart! So even if the sun is high in the sky, I just can't make up my mind to find out ... I'd rather die of grief in this bed. The house still has its shutters closed; I meet old F; he must have heard the shot and looks at me sadly. My sister, who's getting dressed, says to me, "Why don't you go and take a look among the fir trees?" But I don't answer; I take my head in my hands and sob ... After all, it might have been no more than a morning hunter. Oh, I daren't find out; I don't want to know; yesterday evening he was so wretched.

True Ruin

When I was young, I believed the spirits and fairies troubled themselves to show me the way, and whatever insults were thrown at me, I believed that they were whispering their words to others, which had no aim but my well being and mine alone. The reality and disaster which have made me a singer in this square teach me that I have always been abandoned by the gods. Oh spirits, oh fairies, give me back my illusion today!

Glory, Robbery, or Revolution

We arrived at the top in a posh carriage. Through the trees, we could see the setting sun. The castle had columns and geraniums. It was here we were meant to perform a play that synthesized the whole of Shakespeare's works. Before all that, when it came to me—what bridges I had to cross, walls, turrets! All those people with a pince-nez I bumped into at the top of a tower! Those jewelers! Those ladies! (They dress better here than in Paris!) Finally, evening falls. The hall of Lancashire Castle is a kind of Versailles. The room is packed. The ladies are half Ophelia, half bourgeoise. One gentleman as Romeo looks like a Strasbourg *pâté en croute*: that's me! In the morning, there were some Mounet-Sullys in bedsheets. The next day some friends pushed their way through the glass door and invaded the dining room: they ate all day: the servants were meant to make sure the doors weren't forced open. Was that glory? Robbery? Revolution?

History

The shop's shutters were open like a badly folded fan. That was where the musketeers lived. One was spitting in the ashes, the other was reading the evening paper, the third—that was me—was still lying in bed when the king came in. All you could see was his silhouette. The king brought me a captain's certificate: a laundryman's notepad on which was written a list of men and objects to be supplied in order to be a captain. Moreover, I would be called Charles de France in the future, and that got me thinking on more than one point. The next day two charming four-year-olds arrived with rifles: they were the guards: I sat them on my lap.

Life and Tide

There are times when I don't know what light enabled me to glimpse the crest of a wave, and on occasion, too, the sound of our instruments didn't cover the din of the approaching ocean. Night at the villa was surrounded by sea. Your voice had the inflexion of a voice from hell, and the piano was no more than the shadow of sound. So, you, calm in your red smock, you touched my shoulder with the end of your bow just as the emotion from the Flood was bringing me to a stop. "Let's start over!" you said. Oh life, oh grief, oh the ache of eternal new beginnings! How many times when the ocean overwhelmed me with necessities have I said, suppressing sorrows which were all too real, alas!—"Let's start over!" And my will was like the villa that dreadful night. The nights hold nothing for me but equinoctial tides.

The Bibliophile

The book's binding is a golden mesh, keeping prisoner cocka-toos of a thousand colors, ships whose sails are postage stamps, sultanesses with decorations of paradise over their heads to show how wealthy they are. The book keeps prisoner heroines who are very poor, steamships which are very black, and poor gray sparrows. The author is a head held prisoner by a big white wall (I refer to his stiff shirtfront).

M. Gilquin and Oriental Poetry

The city is on a hill: all you can see are the minarets. Chariots are descending: they take the shape of minarets being pulled by galloping horses: here's the carpenters' chariot with its turrets, and the others. Mme Gilquin found the key to the temple while saving her cat. Nannies get a thousand children to piss in the lake and we look at objects of art in the windows. What draws my attention? The album with its story of M. and Mme Gilquin written in Chinese ink. Why is M. Gilquin naked? He's pissed into his top hat like the children into the lake. You won't catch me going into that city.

Just to Say Nothing

The barrow of thunder ends up in Spain via a ball of rainbow. In a country where the churches are surrounded by geraniums of all colors, I saw it on a horse's tail.

The light coming from the turning in the passageway is so white. The light comes from the other side. The staircase comes down from opposite the light, but it can't be seen. No! It won't be seen! I alone will be seen from behind on the edge of a step, from behind on the edge of a landing. The walls that are still here in the night won't be seen. Only the hollows that are still here in the night will be seen, the men who are still here in the hollows. The first is cloaked in shadow; he is cloaked in night. The second I haven't seen; I only sense he's there. The third has descended; he has come right up to me. No one else has moved. The one who descended is wearing checked trousers; his hair is over his eyebrows and his hair is black. He has put his hand on his cheek because his cheeks are overripe. He looks like a man of nothing, and he has climbed back into his night, back into his hollow. The light coming from the turning in the passageway is so white, before me, before me. And I realize that these men were those of my books to come.

Old Saxony

I don't know if it's puppet theater or reality. The lady's pretending to be naked because she's eighty and beautiful as a child. She proudly talks about 1720 because we're now in 1780. The door's decorated with artificial flowers and she's been crowned with roses. One carriage has offended her carriage by making it sound as if it were in its sixties. She's laid out on the sofa and asking me for news of my manuscripts, which are illegible. The horses themselves are minuscule and the trees are illegible.

Let's Make the Old Themes New

In a country where the public sale of paintings takes place in a courtyard, the frames were on the ground, and more than three hundred windows were hired out by their owners and were packed with butchers. Just as they would for the guillotine, they'd come to see the execution of art and happiness. Many of the butchers at the windows had binoculars.

The Japanese general is conducting his review of the armies of Europe. His trousers are so long, they hang twisted like a corkscrew over his shoes. In the midst of the armies is a bishop in a lace surplice at a kitchen table. The bishop is plump, with some hairs sticking out of his chin, and his eyes are all watery. The Japanese general is about to severely censure the bishop, but then realizes he's met him elsewhere; he looks at him, salutes, and moves on.

Mawkish Poem

Oh river port, oh somber greens, the boat filled with my friends moved along the stone quay, and only one of them reached out an affectionate hand to me. I have enough friends to populate this mountain with ants, to populate an ocean with triremes and rowers. Oh river port, oh somber greens, the boat wasn't carrying ten of them; they were hidden under the sail which protects the most delicate. They were protected from me. One of them reached out an affectionate hand and it wasn't the one I like best; it was he whom I would willingly forget.

Cosmogony

From his barrel, God (there is a God), watches over Earth. He sees it as so many decaying teeth. My eye is God! My eye is God! The decaying teeth are like an infinitely tiny droplet, which classifies each of them. My heart is God's barrel! My heart is the barrel! The universe is to me as it is to God.

My Life

The town for the taking is in my room. The enemy's plunder isn't heavy, and the enemy won't make off with it since he has no need of money because it's a story and nothing but a story. The town's ramparts are painted wood: we'll cut them out to glue them into our book. There are two chapters or parts. Here is a red king with a gold crown mounting a saw: that's Chapter Two; as for Chapter One, I don't remember it anymore.

Isabelle's Pigs

Before dawn in Moscow—what terrors! The servants were still not dressed in their livery; the kitchen was lit by a gas lamp. Why had I got up in the night? Perhaps I found it poetic, or else I wanted, for once, to see the sun rise over Moscow. The servants were hanging around the kitchen table; a peasant's square bonnet was there, too, and I recognized Isabelle the beggar woman. They gave her a freshly cut loaf of bread, for which she didn't thank them. Going down through the dark suburb, where only one shop had its light on, I crossed paths with Isabelle carrying a big sack, and I said to her:

"You must have a lot of children, my poor Isabelle, to go to such great pains for them."

"Oh no, Monsieur Max, it's for my pigs."

And I went back home; near the sink, my little moujik was gazing over Moscow all cool and fresh from being bathed in the night: I asked him for my eggs, and we carefully tested them in the water to make sure we only got the fresh ones: "The heaviest will be for my lunch, the lightest for Isabelle's pigs."

M. R. K.'s Wallpaper

Hell's ceiling is affixed with big gold nails. Above that, there's the Earth. The eternal flames are huge twisting fountains of light. As for the Earth, there's a small slope: a field of closely mown wheat and a small sky of onion skin, where a cavalcade of frenzied dwarves pass by. On each side, a pine wood and an aloe wood. Mademoiselle Suzanne, you have been summoned before the Revolutionary Tribunal for having discovered a single white hair among your black ones.

True Poem

My older brothers and I would split up near the moats. "Come on, take the knife!"

We were under the pine trees. It was all grass and flowers. "Ah, watch out for the water!"

Sometimes we came back together with a plant in our hands. "It's a poison rose!"

But when we had to look for a pot at home to hold the harvest in, that was something else.

The naval officer slept in his bed, his back to the door.

Our cousin was doing the housework, the sheets were on the chairs. My sisters were singing in the attic, and as for me, with flowers in my hands, I stayed like a small child on the steps of the staircase that was fading away.

Allusion to a Circus Scene ▬▬▬▬▬▬

Green thorn! Green thorn! Her Ladyship is a cowboy; the columns of pines look like ruins. All the birds of the sky (there is no sky) fly toward his musketeer's hat as if it were the sea. And this was going on in New England! A blond youth, overly dressed like a hunter, is complaining that he hasn't eaten for sixteen hours. Her Ladyship will not give him any little birds from the islands: she'll lead him into a cave where he can take off his boots.

Superior Degeneration

The balloon rises, shining, its tip shining even more. Neither the tilted sun, which casts a ray the way a bad monster casts a spell, nor the cries of the crowd—nothing will stop it rising! No! The sky and the balloon are but one spirit: the sky will only open for the balloon. And yet, oh balloon, take heed! Some shadows are shifting in your gondola, oh unfortunate balloon! The balloonists are drunk.

Fearing the Worst ▬▬▬▬▬▬▬▬▬▬▬

He was one of those who think with the back of their head, and he lived in the second courtyard of a house which had no third, a ground floor and none above it. Before agreeing to rent all these empty spaces for free, the landlord wanted to enjoy them himself: he came into the courtyard from the back. His curiosity turned to hate: he regarded the mysterious alcove with its green curtains as a fleas' nest and as a caricature or a poster, a pretentiously cryptic piece of art.

His hate turned to fury when he came across our hero on the other side of the street. He'd followed him to the lodgings of a sick young woman looked after by an old woman with white hair swept back and parted in the middle, whose eyes shone with fear. This stony financier called him "Monsieur Foreskin" because he himself was Jewish. Ah, what a frightful life began then! One night he was woken by four shady, loutish persons who claimed they were the tenants of his own room and tried to kick him out. Other times they played some appalling tricks on him. And so, panic-stricken, he got himself a revolver: the owner was living in a detached part of the house where his daughter kept her musician friends. One Sunday he put a ladder against the rose espalier wall, wanting to kill his enemy: it was he who wound up rolling in the flowerbed with a hole in his face.

The Sky's Mystery

Having returned from the ball, I sat by the window and contemplated the sky: it seemed to me that the clouds were the great heads of old men sitting at a table and that a white bird decorated with its own feathers was being brought to them. A great river crossed the sky. One of the old men lowered his eyes to me. He was even about to speak when the enchantment fell away, leaving the pure stars twinkling.

Silence in Nature

When we used to go bird-hunting in the wooded hills of Finistère, my dog and I, Rataud enjoyed himself along the way making figures of eight around my footsteps; the faster I moved the more he got excited, and his joy was crazy when I ran. Rataud was a fox terrier. He had a black patch on his left ear and another on his tail.

The gulf's beach—I cannot see the end of it. The sea's sands—I cannot see any trace of my footprints there. And this house at the foot of the cliff (ah, the most beautiful of the century)—alas, I cannot see its torchlights of granite, nor its ledges of fitted stone. I see nothing but one floor more each time I turn my head.

◊

The child took me by the hand, and I protected him against misfortune. Who could his mother be? Whom should I return him to? The laundrywoman spoke to me of ninety francs on the stove she was cleaning. "Here's another child," she told me. "This one's circumcised like you." She threw a small figure from the Massacre of the Innocents onto the mat.

Praise

How do we hang the wreaths to the wood of his remains if not with butcher hooks? One inscription reads: "To my spirit—the Little Lighthouse of the West." Another has: "To my eloquence— the Little Parisian." Another: "To his character, replete with amiability—friends of the Departed." Oh no! Not that! There's something shameful about dressing up a carcass.

The Truth about Latude

A great deal has been written about the case of Latude, but not the truth. It was to shield herself from her own heart that Madame de Pompadour, that gracious Napoleon of love, had the little blue and white officer locked up in the Bastille. Latude escapes! Where's he heading? To the country of Spinoza. But he realized that the taste for meditation could only satisfy him in towers, and he returned to his little hole of love.

Pierrot Has No Right to a Statue ═══════════

The two temples face each other across the very narrow street,
and there's an interchange of great columns, of entrances and
flagstones, of Doric roofing. Who would have believed that
such a tight spot in a suburb would be chosen for a parade?
Some bearded Greeks in red cool themselves on the steps with
golden fans, and Black Pierrot, dressed up in the blue ribbon of
the Order of the Holy Spirit, like a cute Henri III, at the foot of
the grand doorway, seeing the street congested with pedestals
and statues, wonders whether one of those empty pedestals is
not meant for him.

Contagion, or Imitation

Full of daydreams, both of us, let's go down rue des Boucheries. The pavement's dry, the sun's shining. We're off to see, my mother and I, the joiner's daughter, who's gone mad. The joiner's little home has only one floor. There are two beds in the two rooms. Let's go! The birds sing in their cages and the windows only let in as much light as the Virginia Creeper allows. In the first bed is a madwoman, in the second there's another sick one. Ah, my God, with what dreadful reverence they welcome us in. A lady has disguised herself as a sister of mercy; a smock takes the place of a headdress; she's attired in a red fluffy blouse with the sleeves hanging loose; the old girl sings in an astonishing voice, one that is too loud and that I don't recognize in her, the voice of a man, and the mother, smiling, pours out some large glasses of cognac. The real madwoman watches from the other room, her elbow on the wood of the bed, calm and sure of herself.

Japanese Family

After the death and burial of his sister, the little Japanese man left for France! The little Japanese man! He will never forget his sister! He's an illustrator for comic magazines, but to him all the faces of the women he draws are those of his beloved sister. An old Japanese woman from the embassy thinks she'll make him happy by sending the comics to his father back home. The father breaks into sobs: he's recognized his beloved daughter.

Tale

In the valley so lovely, oh! I would like to tell you the motto of its continuous cone rocks, the valley with its trees so lovely, the profile of the ogress whose earrings were from your castle, Chinon—its outer staircase! She'd eaten the little black rider, but not the chain binding the prisoner to the black horse's tail. She was afraid the chain would give her toothache, so made do with the first rat that came her way: that's what making her grimace.

It was not far from Lorient. The sun shone brightly and we used to go strolling, and as the September days went by, we watched as the sea rose, rose and covered the woods, the landscapes, the cliffs. Very soon all that remained to resist the blue sea were the meandering paths under the trees, and the families came closer together. Among us was a child dressed in a sailor's suit. He was sad and took hold of my hand: "Monsieur," he said, "I've been to Naples—do you know that in Naples there are lots of little streets; in those streets you can be all alone without anyone seeing you. It's not that there aren't a lot of people in Naples, but there are so many little streets that there is never more than one street for each person." "What tales is he still telling you, this child," the father said, "he's never been to Naples." "Monsieur, your son is a poet." "That's fine, but if he turns out to be a literary hack, I'll wring his neck!" The meandering paths left dry by the sea had made him dream of the streets of Naples.

Versatility, Impotence, and Traditional Education ▬

He'd had the spoilt thirty-year-old child put in a child's high-chair. His brother was making a speech: "No business should employ anyone overeducated because he'll lack humility. What have you done with Marcel? I can hear his parents moaning and I can hear very different kinds of moaning going on. Did you know that Joseph Dumain knows a thousand lines of poetry by heart as well as the sermons of Boussuet?" "The titles!" said his mother. "What? The titles? Okay then, the name of Joseph is synonymous with impotence." The thirty-year-old spoilt child climbed up into his highchair: he was crying for himself; his father was crying, too. After a moment, the spoilt child was in the corridor, laughing, and said: "There's a half-truth in what he says, but only half." His brother added: "But just take a look at yourself!" "After this war, everything will change." "Why after rather than while?"

Our Poor Man's Pleasures

From here the orchestra is nothing more than the crackle of crickets in the grass. Despite the wooden wall, this is not an arena for bullfighting. The amphitheater is glazed. It's like a joiner's workshop seen from the street. Democracy is under glass. "Lean over a little more, hatless woman. If the actors are on the far left side, you will see their brown doublets, like two bugs at the foot of your bed." This is how it is along the fortifications of cities; this is how it is for all those on the edge of disgrace, misery, and death.

The Patron's Delicate Role ═══════════

On the Exhibition's stairway, there's a large rug but the huge paintings on the wall were out of fashion before they were finished.

On the Exhibition's stairway, there are three pink hats which are also in the paintings.

On the Exhibition's stairway, there's a stingy gentleman who agrees to support the upkeep of a magazine and its two contributors.

On the Exhibition's stairway, there are lots of big dogs: they've got white teeth and white eyes and they dream only of devouring you, but their master sometimes intervenes: he's a Japanese missionary.

Down in hell, Dante and Virgil were inspecting a brand-new barrel. Dante walked around it. Virgil mulled over it. Yet it was just a barrel of smoked herring. Eve, lovely as ever, still lives in that place, bowed down with despair, even if in her nakedness she has the consolation of a halo. Pinching her nose, Eve declared, "Oh boy, that smells bad!" and moved away.

They are not roses in a field, they're the faces of his admirers. His horse's saddle is a tiger skin. The Japanese women, dressed with a single stroke of the quill, carry sparkly clean jars, and the sun is transformed into a tree, but look, the horse's saddle stretches out and scratches all the roses and the horse and the Japanese women, and everything disappears, and this hydra itself is no more than a tiger skin for the bare rider, who is just an old man in tears praying. The stroke of the quill for the Japanese women has melted into the tree; nothing remains except the jars on the tiger skin.

An Israelite Literary Man

The bill from the tailor is the same as the one from the doctor: the shop I don't know, but the staircase and the man I do. On the staircase I meet my cousins. What! Still so young! One has to go back inside in spite of the hubbub. Everyone is at the table and the fat mother makes a sign to Pierre to kiss me: "Oh, with pleasure, my child!" Cousin Bertha is very ugly, but she was once beautiful: work's the cause of that. Don't believe it: age is the cause! She's never done anything except be beautiful. Everyone's embarrassed into silence. I'm the first to break it: "What's the difference between a tailor and a doctor?" They laugh. In my family the tailors are doctors and vice versa. We talk about Macedonia. The Macedonian road where I held my little sister's hand if they hunted Jews because Jews slaughtered too many fat calves. Here, there's no longer any difference between a tailor and a doctor: a fattened calf is slaughtered every day. And me, I'm just a poor, well-meaning person they keep company with out of habit, even on the road to Macedonia.

The Devil's Tricks to Recapture His Victim ▬▬

The dark quay, in the triangular keep, bristling with winter plane trees, lovely skeletons on the sky's low neckline. A beautiful but flat-chested woman, who lived in the hotel with us, hid her hair under a wig or some black satin. One day, on top of the stonework, she appeared to me in the full sunlight of the sea: too big—like the rocks nearby—she was putting on her nightshirt, and I could see that she was a man, and I said so. In the night, on a kind of London wharf, I was chastised: dodge the knife to the face, get your thumb wounded, counterattack with a dagger in the chest at shoulder blade height! The hermaphrodite wasn't dead! Help! Help! They're coming . . . some men—what do I know? My mother! And I see once more the hotel room without any locks on the door: there were, thank God, some hooks, but what spite on the part of the hermaphrodite: a way opens into the attic, a white shutter moves, and the hermaphrodite comes down from there.

Not Exactly Flattering Portraits

The subject of the competition set by my brother for his broth-
ers is the image of Christ on the cross. The youngest prompts
these words: "Oh, that's some anatomy!" I reveal some cub-
ist Christs with their members hanging to the ground from
a height of three meters. "Max researched his anatomies yes-
terday!" they tell me. The style comes from looking through
illustrated dictionaries: there I see at least twenty kinds of cross:
some double, others triple, still others back-to-front. Christ in
his glory on one of them, otherwise elsewhere. There are also
some colossal feet: *the stone feet belonging to the Christ* from
the village of O. And yet, there was no more than one Christ:
which of these images has he chosen?

The Poet's House

He's died and here are his widow and two sons: "It was in this window that we'd see his old man's silhouette, alas!" said the widow. "A marriage for love! What courage, what genius! Our parents consented to everything!" The house has new tenants: a woman was hanging out her washing in the attic: I called out to her, she replied with a few bawdy epithets; an Alsatian dog stared me down; in the garden were roses, withered. New tenants moved in; there was a tiled roof over the steps, and we drank some iced drinks in the garden. What will happen next in the poet's house? Maybe a crime … And you, poor thing, what can you expect from your house, if not treachery from your best friends?

The House of the Guillotined ▬▬▬▬▬

To Paimpol! You cross the hills in the evening. The roofs of the new houses in evening blue and sea blue. A room at the hotel for so many from the smart set. Now for a life of great pursuits. All these little bladders on the sidewalk come from pretend rabbits: a servant blows them up and we take a shot at them: there is but one true rabbit: he's old and seated: "Where's René?" "He puts in an appearance from time to time." René puts rubber soles on his shoes to act out the role of the old rabbit, and we sit down at the table facing Paimpol, facing the port and the evening hills. There's a lady who knows the hostess's secret: "It was in Paimpol last year at this time that . . ." The lady rises, her eyes full of tears. What a scene!

References for an Apprenticeship in Painting

You must pass your high school diplomas! Mme S has gone crazy: so many young painters in one room! You must pass your high school diplomas! Where are my books? Will I have to retake both of them? In that case, I've wasted another two years! You must pass your high school diplomas! M. Matisse is dying in a room: "So teach my younger brother drawing since he's watching over you!" But no! If my high school diplomas don't count, don't I have my law degree, which presupposes them? There are iron beds in my messy room. I slept at a friend's. Mme S has gone crazy. It's essential my degree certificate hasn't gotten lost. Oh, thank God for that! I would have wasted another two years preparing for my high school diplomas. For you know, don't you, that I'm useless at Latin.

We Saw It, yet It's Impossible

It's a really small town, but it has a river; for river say "river-bank." On this bank—deserted—there's a small hotel which belonged to a widow: one very narrow floor and some attic rooms, and wrought iron balconies. It's been transformed into a public library with no books. I used to go to work there on a vast table, the worse for wear and painted black. One evening the bailiff said to me: "There are new goings-on up there." There were new goings-on: several characters from the Revolution were seated round my table. Mirabeau was not as ugly as they say he was: he has the neck of an adolescent, and the whole strength of his face is in his mouth: Vergniaud had . . . but I won't describe my astonishment! On the second floor, I found Diderot on a mantelpiece, but shrunk right down. He was naked under a bathrobe and chatting with Mme Rachilde from the *Mercure de France*. Nobody wanted to believe in my revenants. The next day I joined up with a friend and introduced him to those shades. The day after that, he didn't want to acknowledge these realities even though my introductions were made according to the regulations.

On Painting before All Else[7]

Only a few friends and I knew about the affair. Mme de X, a young bride, lived in a castle on the river, six kilometers out of town. One day, Mme X, accused by her husband of adultery, unjustly or not, took her own life. The funeral service was conducted in a chapel in a hollow in the rocks of the town. The port is situated in a quincunx of ancient trees in the hollow of a valley. A three-masted ship was waiting for the deceased to bear her to the castle cemetery. The priests, few and in a hurry, and some high-society ladies, filed along the foot of the rocky mount before the three-master. A few curious folk were present at the loading of the coffin, which, laid on the grass, was watched over by the ladies in their grand funeral attire. Now a hatless, romantic-looking man seemed to be brandishing a black medallion. He raised his arms very high: "I was wrong." And I realized that the coffin had been opened and the romantic man was the husband, who was rather ugly in spite of his long hair and long beard. She had the face of a frivolous Englishwoman; death had not ennobled her. It seems that at this very moment the guilty party presumed responsible for the entire drama, a certain high-school tutor, having to give his pupils a lesson, drank so much to blot out all thought of the dead woman that he had to be carried away, dead drunk, much to the amusement of the schoolboys. Walking under the beech trees of the green little port in the company of my sister whose life was to become so troubled, we reached the countryside. What can we make out of this story from the point of view of art? My sister is asking for some pencils and a sketchbook as soon as possible.

On Dilettantism before All Else ▰▰▰▰▰▰▰

In the antiques shop, frequented by the friends of Anatole France, you need to scramble over many corners of chests with resoluteness and faith. Everyone's going to take me for a fool: a big female Hindu head . . . why female? Written in blue thread on stuffed elephant heads, and repeated ad infinitum, we have: "You are going to tear open the great . . . the great . . . Arethusian!" (In the style of Ana, of ananas, of an anatomist . . .) What contortions! And the lewd Jew, here! Oh, it's written on a Buddhist trinket jewel! I scramble about everywhere: old goose feathers, broken jugs, paintings of the time, a big female Hindu head, big female Hindu head. How much? I daren't ask the price. Finally, the goddess smiles, the pretty little tongue-in-cheek face much too alive to be made of ivory: she was there on the Buddhist trinket, and I hadn't seen her . . . That's what it's like to look for nothing but old bottles for Paul.

A Bit of Modernism by Way of Conclusion ▬▬▬

Lit up in diamonds in the inky night, half the World Fair of 1900 recoils from the Seine and collapses in a single block because a crazy poet's head in Heaven's school is biting a diamond star.

A Grieving, Final Appeal to Phantom Muses of the Past

I was born near a racetrack where I used to see horses racing under the trees. Oh, my trees! My horses! For it was all for me! I was born near a racetrack! My name was traced by my childhood in the bark of chestnut trees and beeches. Alas, all that remains of my trees are the white feathers of a bird which cries out, "Léon! Léon!" Oh, hazy memories of splendid chestnut trees on which as a child I carved my grandfather's name! Hazy memories of races! Jockeys! They're now just poor little toys seen from far away. There's nothing noble about the horses now and my jockeys are helmeted in black. Go on! Go around and around! Old, trapped thoughts which will never take flight. The befitting symbol is not the buoyant gallop of jockeys in the green, but some dusty bas-relief which would hide from my grief the autumn chestnut trees on which my grandfather's name is written.

A Philosophical Return to That Which Is No More ▬

After adolescence, we no longer know rapture, but we can know joy. Hiding the holes in your socks, either one or the other! Being worried about missing the train! Having just enough money for the trip and at the last moment your still-sleeping brother has doubled the cost! Perhaps these raptures come from the fact that apprehensions and hesitations bring more worry when we haven't had any experience of anything. Won't I be having some love affair in Nantes? For love, read pistol, and I didn't have a pistol. Now what surprised me most on this trip was to find myself recognized at a cobbler's because of my resemblance to an old relative and the praise I heard of this person whose life to me seemed insignificant. Young people take everything seriously even though they don't know how to be serious about what it is they're taking. Truth be told, the emotions they put into it are out of proportion.

It was no more than a Neapolitan nativity play. The light was cast on the cloak of a doll with a fox's head and policeman's cap. The fox was asking Oedipus questions in a patronizing manner. "Aren't you going to answer me, Oedipus?" "Have you paid me for that?"

Exhortation for the Future

My brother the African is a sculptor. We're in an attic, working on a bas-relief, a portrait of Simon, the patriarch of the Moabites, his hands crossed, holding a figure of Christ. I correct the hands a little too much ... here they are, carved out. The patriarch didn't have them like that! The composition is simple. I make the observation that the two lines in the shape of raised arms shouldn't start haphazardly, and here we are now sizing them up with rulers. Meanwhile, we're expected in the main studio. An Israelite artist is there, and I remark that all the bas-reliefs have admirable Phoenician heads. Shall we sit at the table? That's the way Rodin thinks, isn't it? No, but it's a sham of the same sort! Ah, my mother, how happy I am! Nowhere like the provinces for work! I wrote a sermon, a letter, a thesis on Simon, the patriarch of the Moabites, and persuaded my brother that instead of sculpting for a few dimes, he should be spreading the good news in taverns.

Papers to recopy with better handwriting! The imperial palace at night, rooms to sleep in! One has a red and blue bed! Over there! Over there the emperor is having a massage, and the empress, pale and motionless under her canopy, receives me without a word. The palace is busiest when the servants turn down the bedcovers, and here is the English governess with her wide, staring eyes and her bags which keep having to be redone, like my papers.

The keep is new, its paving stones swept clean by the air, you know . . . Squatting in bottle shards, the king of spades has thin legs but a big head, and the basket for his crown awaits, accepting. The iron door, oh witches, oh magic! Oh, pointed teeth in diabolic smiles and . . . (let's just say: Shakespearean) the iron door catches daylight from above. Bracabas was thinking about the keep before him. A young kitchenhand passing by made a ball out of his newspaper for the crown-basket. And there you have it. More children, more kings! And the king of spades, a very decent gentleman, innocently attended the council meeting with *Le Constitutionnel* on his head and over his meek shoulders. He lost his Civil List, poor man! They were just waiting for the opportunity to dispose of it.

A Bit of Theosophy, Unforeseen but Not Unforeseeable

The fortifications are whiter and farther away. One can no longer make out the doors. It's time to think of my dead child. Divorced, remarried, I'm a widower and I remember. O exquisite face of my first wife! She was blonde, she had the innocent air of those who have not suffered.

O angelic figure of our child: our dead child! Many evenings have I seen in my mind the burial of that child. All the evils followed that hearse: those that affect the stomach, those that affect the forehead, those that affect the thigh, those that affect the foot. Moreover, there were some missing an arm, some lame, some on crutches, and some blind.

Weep over your deceased wives! Weep over your beautiful, dead child. You would weep with less suffering if the procession did not lead even the gargoyles of Notre-Dame to the graveyard.

THE DICE CUP: ADDE[9]

It's since he had a family that HRH feels exiled. Out of delicacy, she doesn't want to leave him, and he doesn't want to go in disguise to the border and flee. Slippers. Two brothers-in-law at the windows all day long, watching the crinoline dresses and the children's hoops.

A prisoner by his own word and under the moved hand of beech trees, what destiny does he dream of? Empires? He's dreaming of having a collar button purchased in Basel.

Meeting with a visitor "of the night," a pal of the servant who was none other than . . . Playing chess with the one whose identity he doesn't know.

Afraid in the night of being assassinated genealogically.

During the day, of course, strolls by the lake; the archduke takes the oars and pushes off with his foot from the shores of Europe. In any case, she's no longer thinking about him. He scribbles down some lines of poetry.

The Toxic Life of Our Provinces

The eraser to erase your hours.
　　　The eraser to erase your dreams.
　　　The eraser to erase your hunters' trails.
　　　The eraser to erase your wrinkles.
　　　A mask of hair for our regrets.

Colonial Exposition ▬▬▬▬▬▬▬▬▬

The legs of mangroves look like those of Arabian horses in battalions.

◊

My husband is honest, I'm smart and honest, yet I'm just a puppet.

◊

It wasn't worth cutting off the clown's head to show that the fair was over—the corpse itself was enough, and that ticking gilet.

◊

The classy thing was to go swimming in a swanky swimsuit to prove you didn't use the same one twice.

◊

We were expecting the Empress Eugenie to appear as Marie-Antionette. It was the costume of Joan of Arc she'd chosen.

◊

At night, Harpagon's nocturnal shadow examines my drawings.

◊

A man becomes spiritual through passion and experience. A woman's spirit remains that of the fashion of her time.

◊

From the keyboard of its abdomen, the bee draws black and yellow sounds.

◊

The automobile had the shape of a crinoline, or a crinkly moon, and the children who came running had the skullcaps of pierrots.

◊

A row of trees take their little ones to escape the fire. Finally, they let their arms fall, disheartened. They'd learned the sorrow of being trees.

◊

We'd had numerous dinners, one of which was exclusively diplomatic. Everyone was diplomatic, and there was even an embassy attaché.

◊

The seismograph! The seismograph to measure my earth tremors.

◊

The half-disk of this necktie, cosmic circle the only frame worthy of your face.

◊

The flesh deformed by its humiliations says to the flesh overflowing with its ecstasies: "I don't recognize you anymore." "It's just that I'm myself now," answers the accomplice.

◊

My clothes on the chair were a puppet, a dead puppet.

◊

MECHANICAL MUSIC
IN A BISTRO

Edgar Poe's raven has a halo which he extinguishes from time to time.

◊

The poor man inspected Saint Martin's mantle and said: "No pockets?"

◊

Adam and Eve were born in Quimper.

◊

Why dispatch this watermelon to Adolphe? Is it an insult? Hey, my name's not Adolphe! Why did she announce her suicide to me? Did she know I loved her?

◊

In the old days we went to rue de la Paix
in a coupé
for our babe and her babay.
Nowadays they're coupons
for Baby we cut out and display
when we're not too put upon.

◊

Title of a large picture in a small museum: "To congratulate the sailors on their shipwreck, Kind Louis XVI, in uniform, climbed down the rope ladder." Government Gift.

◊

The basket which had brought Saint Paul down from the ramparts found itself filled with miraculous flowers, and the rope was treated like that of a gallows.

◊

Bronze leggings and colored beads, the whole country was orange.

◊

A poet said it: a woman has her good points, with all her faults.
    "Put in your baskets,
    shepherds, these birds,
    these cocks, these hens."
    A sage also said (this sage was a Hindu):
    "The female of the sacred Apis bull is sweetest.
    Indra, woman of the sky, make it rain on us!"
    "This heavy load is too much for our little ships."
    "But keep in mind the cow's two wings."

◊

A princess once lived in a quarter slice of pear.

◊

It took more spirit for this poor youth to come to you, lady, to hear himself say that he is a fool, than it takes for you to upstage him and say that you believe him such.

◊

The salmon has pink flesh because he feeds on shrimp.

◊

In the Parc Monceau, under the carriage entrance to the palace, there was a little prince, just fourteen, so anemic that he wrote in pink ink. In another palace, there was another little prince. They never met each other. In the sky was an ogre opening his mouth.

TRANSLATOR'S NOTES

As a translator I have done my utmost to convey the wonderful playfulness and rich ambiguities of Max Jacob's prose poems. However, it has to be admitted that there is much wordplay and punning that cannot be replicated in translation. It is hoped that this translation will inspire readers to seek out the original French.

Regarding problematic language and attitudes occasionally on display throughout this collection, the publisher and I decided to maintain such details in the translation and keep the book situated in its time.

1. Jacob's novel, *Filibuth ou la montre en or*, was published in 1923.

2. In some editions, this sequence has been mistakenly presented as part of "The Cock and the Pearl." See Antonio Rodriguez's note in Max Jacob, *Œuvres* (Paris: Éditions Gallimard, 2012), 1760.

3. *La Pèlerine ecossaise* by Sacha Guitry, a popular play, had its debut performance on 15 January 1914.

4. Italian (in Max Jacob's version of it): "the space of the Kiss" and "Bacchus in the heart."

5. A play on the title of Flaubert's novel, *L'Éducation sentmentale* (1869).

6. This prose poem quotes and plays with the opening stanza of Baudelaire's poem, "L'invitation au voyage."

7. The titles of this prose poem and the one following play on "De la musique avant toute chose," the opening line of Verlaine's poem, "Art poétique."

8. A play on Mallarmé's sonnet, "Le vierge, le vivace et le bel aujourd'hui."

9. Adde or addendum: a homophone for "à dés" of the book's French title. This section of additional prose poems appeared in *La Nouvelle Revue Française*, 219, in December 1931. Max Jacob added these poems in 1943 at the same time as he wrote "A Short History of *The Dice Cup*." Various editions of *Le cornet à dés* with contents added or deleted

have been published over the years. See endnotes 74 and 75 in Jacob, *Œuvres*, 1763, and Étienne-Alain Hubert's 2003 "Note sur le texte" in Jacob, *Le Cornet à dés*, 268–270.

Ian Seed's translations include *The Thief of Talant* (Wakefield Press, 2016), the first translation into English of Pierre Reverdy's radical experiment in poetry and narrative, *Le voleur de Talan* (1917). He has written four collections of prose poetry: *The Underground Cabaret* (2020), *New York Hotel* (2018), *Identity Papers* (2016), and *Makers of Empty Dreams* (2014), all published by Shearsman Books. Reviewing *New York Hotel* in the Times Literary Supplement, Mark Ford commented: "Seed's micro-narratives and oblique parables are at once droll and haunting, as unpredictable as quicksand, and as elegant as the work of those masters of the prose poem, Max Jacob and Pierre Reverdy." He teaches at the University of Chester in the UK.